Other book published by this author

Leadership Defined

PRIDE AND DISCIPLINE

The Hallmarks of a United States Marine

Colonel Donald J. Myers, USMC (Ret)

Order this book online at www.trafford.com
or email orders@trafford.com

Most Trafford titles are also available at major online book retailers.

Printed in the United States of America.

ISBN: 978-1-4907-3636-5 (sc)
ISBN: 978-1-4907-3639-6 (hc)
ISBN: 978-1-4907-3640-2 (e)

Library of Congress Control Number: 2014908821

Trafford rev. 06/16/2014

www.trafford.com

North America & international
toll-free: 1 888 232 4444 (USA & Canada)
fax: 812 355 4082

CONTENTS

Pre-Introduction ix
Foreword xi
Introduction xv

Chapter 1 The Beginning 1
Chapter 2 Why Abuse 20
Chapter 3 The Drill Instructor 30
Chapter 4 Initial Changes 36
Chapter 5 The Studies 44
Chapter 6 The Schedule 47
Chapter 7 The Regiment 52
Chapter 8 Individual Combat Training and Rifle Range 56
Chapter 9 Stress Management 60
Chapter 10 Stories 64
Chapter 11 Goals 83
Chapter 12 Why We Are Different 91
Chapter 13 Changes and Results 94
Epilogue 103

Dedicated to all Marines, past, present, and future,
especially the drill instructors,
who are the most instrumental in making new Marines.

As long as there is a Marine Corps,
there will be a United States of America.

PRE-INTRODUCTION

Colonel Don Myers knows Marine Corps recruit training. As you will read, he was a recruit. Thirty years later he commanded the recruit training regiment at Marine Corps Recruit Depot, Parris Island, South Carolina. Between those years, he trained and led Marines, graduated from the Naval Academy, and continued to train and lead Marines—in garrison and combat.

We served under Colonel Myers when he commanded the recruit training regiment at Parris Island 1982-1984. He was an engaged commander. He walked around. His presence was known. He talked to drill instructors. He talked to the officers, all of them, in the battalions. Most importantly, Colonel Myers listened. Colonel Myers not only knew recruit training, he knew what was going on in his regiment.

It is only now, thirty years removed from our experiences, that we are able to fully understand the significance of our time at Parris Island. With time comes clarity. Lacking the breadth and depth of Colonel Myers's experience and wisdom, it is not our task in this brief introduction to address each aspect of recruit training that he so thoroughly covers. Rather, decades of reflection have brought clarity to something we do know about—the critical role of officer supervision while drill instructors are making Marines. And that is a key variable that flows throughout this book.

During our years in the regiment, Second Recruit Training Battalion 1983-1986, the model for recruit training was barely more than a handful of years old following the 1976 Congressional hearings about recruit abuse (namely the pugil sticks-beating death of Recruit Lynn E. McClure at Recruit Depot, San Diego). Those hearings came twenty years after the disastrous and tragic Ribbon Creek incident at Parris Island where six recruits drowned during a disciplinary march. Ribbon Creek caused the Corps to assign junior officers to supervise recruit training. The series commander billet was created.

Just twenty years later, as part of the 1976 hearings and to save the very existence of Marine Corps recruit training, General Louis H. Wilson promised the Congress he would increase officer supervision. He doubled the role of officers—that is, two officers per series and commanding and executive officers at the company, battalion, and regiment. In short, if a series was out of the rack, an officer would be present and supervising. Commanding officers and their executive officers walked around.

Supervision did not end there. The Commandant also ordered two general officers assigned to each recruit depot and that a general officer would always be aboard the depot. The generals, too, walked around.

Now, more than thirty-one years after first reporting for duty and following a couple of recent visits to Parris Island, we've noticed not much has changed as to the philosophy and approach to training recruits. The Corps still makes Marines the way it used to—performance in battle stands as proof. But frankly and as it should be, there's much, in training and with facilities, that is better.

However, one disturbing change caught our attention: where are the officers—namely the lieutenants and the second general officer? Has officer supervision returned to that of post-Ribbon Creek but pre-1976 hearings days?

Thirty-eight years ago, the Congress did not have a sense of humor as they listened to testimony of horror. Only their faith in the commandant of the Marine Corps and a few of his generals saved recruit training (which Marines know indeed saved the Marine Corps). Another serious incident that could have been prevented by appropriate officer supervision will likely not fall upon sympathetic ears. To lose recruit training would be the certain death of our Corps.

Marines, regardless of generation, upon reading Colonel Myers's book, will pause and think about their recruit training experience; it's life-changing. Marines who lived through the Ribbon Creek days and post-1976 hearings will surely remember the increased role of officers in recruit training. And the importance of their presence validated time and again.

Today's Marines, especially officers, will be well-served to carefully read this book, not just about recruit training but about common-sense leadership, to understand the history of recruit training and contemplate if less officer supervision is worth the risk—to recruit, to drill instructor, to Corps, to country.

A. F. Weddington
Colonel, USMC (Retired)

R. H. Barrow
Lieutenant Colonel, USMC (Retired)

FOREWORD

Tom Peters examined countless organizations in his books about management (leadership) and suggested that the techniques were transferable to other areas. This is merely one of those areas where they were transferred, and they worked.

Although the examples used involve the training of Marine recruits at Parris Island, South Carolina, the techniques employed are equally appropriate to schools, universities, businesses, and government agencies. People respond to leadership and positive reinforcement the same as Marines.

It makes little difference whether the leader is civilian or military. Leadership principles apply. In a civilian organization, the cost associated with poor leadership may result in bankruptcy; however, in the military it will probably result in blood.

The fundamental tenants in Peters's philosophy demand producing quality by listening and encouraging workers, being innovative, encouraging initiative, and walking around. It is so simple that it is missed. People read it and say, "I knew that." The major difficulty is that although they know it, they do not consistently practice it. They fail to believe that it can be that simple. It is!

The major thread, which weaves its way throughout this book, is that communications are critical and that the leader must take the time to ensure that everyone is aware of why procedures or routines are practiced.

When that is consistently executed along with making sure that employees are treated properly and told why, then all else falls into place. People generally want to perform well and need only the opportunity and encouragement to do it.

Along with communications comes concern for people and their ideas. Allowing and encouraging workers to participate in the effective functioning of the organization reaps huge rewards. Marines respond the same as their civilian counterparts.

The Marines have been a very special part of American society since their beginning on November 10, 1775. It is because of this that what they do as Marines or old Marines makes news. They are expected to be tough, professional, and demanding. These expectations apply particularly in how the Corps goes about the task of making new Marines. The criticism can be very vocal if there appears to be an easing in those demands or toughness.

There has been criticism over the years, with the present no exception, by individuals who felt that Boot Camp was not as tough as the past. This toughness can be legitimate or it can be the code word for maltreatment. Recruits of today must conduct more physical training, learn more academics, undergo closer supervision, and reach higher standards than in other times.

Boot Camp is tough, but fortunately, the brutality often associated with it in the past is disappearing. Brutality does not make it tough but only brutal. The stress of becoming a Marine remains; however, it is not the excessive effective-reducing stress that apparently crept into the training in the late '40s or early '50s.

A recruit need not give up his dignity to become a Marine, and an individual who feels that he must strip a man of that dignity is not much of a leader. These new Marines are disciplined and the indicators that we have historically used to measure discipline show it: unauthorized absences, nonjudicial punishment, courts martial, drug abuse, and early discharges are significantly lower than during the '70s and early '80s. In addition to these measurable areas, one can sense a significant change in the attitudes of these new Marines.

Marine leaders in the operating forces will go out of their way to make it as good as they possibly can for their Marines—not easy, but good. They feel, and rightfully so, that the training should be tough but fair. Why is it that some of these same leaders will go out of their way to make it as nasty as possible for the recruits? For the most part, it is counterproductive and unfair to do so. Boot Camp must not be easy, but it must be fair and conducted with dignity. That was the philosophy of the Commandant, General Robert H. Barrow, and they were the marching orders for my tenure as the commanding officer of the Recruit Training Regiment at Parris Island, South Carolina, from 1982 until 1984.

The drill instructors are more closely screened and trained than ever before. They continue to be the major ingredient in the making of new Marines. Their example by positive leadership is what makes the difference. This book is an effort to show how we went about the task of making new Marines and instilling pride and discipline. It is not the answer but, rather, an answer. The criticism continues, mostly from older Marines who are now retired or completed their active service. They say that Boot Camp is much easier and that the graduates are not disciplined, but it is an emotional argument not supported by fact.

Although much time has elapsed since I first started this book, the tenets remain the same, and the results as seen in Iraq and Afghanistan under combat conditions prove it.

INTRODUCTION

Now that I look back, it doesn't seem possible that so many years have passed since an eighteen-year-old youngster started his career in the Corps. I had wanted to be a military man for as long as I can remember. In fact, my parents would buy me a different uniform each year and I would proudly parade around the neighborhood. Therefore, it came as no surprise when I enlisted in the Marines. I must admit that my folks were quite upset when I quit high school to do so. My dad was especially upset, but he changed his mind four years later as I entered the US Naval Academy from the enlisted ranks as a sergeant.

Boot Camp at Parris Island is not as vivid to me as it is to many others who have written about the subject. The Seventh Battalion was my home, and we lived in eight-man tents. The cursing, hazing, and games were commonplace, but I thought that was part of becoming a Marine. My two junior drill instructors, both Private First Class (PFCs), had less than a year in the Corps. In those days it was not unusual for an individual to graduate from Boot Camp and then return immediately as a drill instructor. We have since learned that there are better ways to make drill instructors, and that practice has been discontinued.

After what seemed to be an eternity, the big day finally arrived in November 1953, when I graduated as the honor man of the platoon. During the next several years, I served as an infantryman in the First and Third Divisions in Japan, Korea, and California. I was promoted to corporal a year after Boot Camp and to sergeant a year later.

There has been a continuous mythology about Boot Camp in an effort to explain why the Marines generally performed so well in combat. The stories about the treatment have been covered in countless fiction and nonfiction books. Many of the stories grow with age, but the reality of success in combat is true. It all adds to the legend and mystique of the Corps. Marine Boot Camp has had two significant investigations concerning recruit maltreatment. The first was McKeown in 1956, and the second, McClure in 1975.

When the McKeown incident occurred in 1956, I was a sergeant in the Third Battalion, Fifth Marines and had been a noncommissioned officer (NCO) since 1954. McKeown was a drill instructor (DI) at Parris

Island who took his platoon on an unauthorized night march in the swamps, which resulted in the drowning of six recruits. I recall vividly my thoughts at the time. *A drill instructor had a platoon of recruit goof-offs and was attempting to instill a little discipline by going through the swamps. A few of the recruits did not listen, and as a result, they drowned. Now, because of a few shit birds, we will be required to change Boot Camp and never be able to instill discipline again.* That was the thought process of a twenty-year-old non-high school graduate sergeant with three years' experience. Now as a colonel over fifty with more than thirty years' experience and only a few credits remaining for a doctorate degree, I can say unequivocally that the sergeant was wrong. There is no place for brutality in the Corps. It does not instill discipline but, rather, the opposite.

There are those who will argue with the philosophy of this book. I am sorry for that. There is only one way to make a Marine, and that is the right way. There is no room in our Corps for those who feel that they need not obey orders or that they can make up their own rules.

The Corps is an elite organization, which requires, demands, and expects discipline from its members. That is the hallmark of a Marine, and it all starts in Boot Camp.

It will be the rare Marine who does not recall the name of his drill instructor; that particular Marine made an indelible mark on his recruits. It has always been so, and it will always remain so. He is the key ingredient in the making of a new Marine. My drill instructor was Sergeant Giles, and PFCs Sullivan and Stennet were his assistants.

As the commanding officer of the Recruit Training Regiment at Parris Island, South Carolina, I personally spoke to approximately nine hundred DIs at various times in groups of no larger than eight and often one-on-one. I found only seven who either did not see, or were not themselves victims of, abuse during their own Boot Camp. It depended on when they went through Boot Camp exactly what happened, but the hazing, cursing, grabbing, punching, and initiation were there.

This is a very important concept because it parallels other types of behavior, which we have studied for years. Alcoholics generally come from families of alcoholics. That is to say that there was a lot of drinking in the family; the father, mother, or a brother, sister, or uncle had a drinking problem. That was the role model, which was observed and, unfortunately, followed. An interesting phenomenon is that many who did not become alcoholics themselves *knowingly* married alcoholics. Another example is child abuse. Studies show that 60-70 percent of child abusers themselves were abused as children. One would suspect that those individuals maturing under such conditions and seeing all the pain and heartache resulting from those types of behavior would be the last to follow suit. Nothing could be further from the truth. They are the first!

It makes sense to me that since almost all the DIs had either been exposed, or believed they had, to some type of abuse in Boot Camp, that they would be susceptible to following suit upon becoming a DI. They had become superb NCOs, and they believed that *all* their training in Boot Camp was why. What they did not realize is that they became superb Marines because of all the good things that their DIs and every other leader taught them and in spite of the bad examples.

It is another rather interesting phenomenon that those individuals who advocate the use of unlawful methods—corporal punishment, they call it—in Boot Camp will agree that it is generally not necessary in the operating forces. For one thing, the Marines would not tolerate it. They would fight back by throwing a brick through the NCO's car window or slashing his tires. Also, at the Basic School, where we train all our lieutenants, the games do not occur. No one will challenge the integrity, courage, or discipline of the officer corps as a whole, and yet it does not have the problems associated with recruit training. One may argue that the officers are older and more educated, but what about those recruits who arrive at the depots with a college degree? Should they be treated differently from the norm? The answer is a definite no; there is no reason to treat men other than as men.

This approach may sound a little different from that expected of a Marine, but it will produce—in fact, it does produce—superb Marines who will acquit themselves well in any arena.

The Marines pride themselves with being an elite all-volunteer force; however, that has not always been true. Although the Marines generally were a volunteer unit throughout its history, they did resort to the draft during WWII, Korea, and Vietnam. In addition, many of the volunteers during the draft years were draft motivated and chose to serve in the Marine Corps rather than be inducted. When the draft ended in 1973, the services were not ready for it. The Marine Corps continued to expect the volunteers to walk in, and they didn't. The commandant made a conscious decision at the time to keep the Corps's strength at its present level and that exacerbated the problem. As the draft ended and the recruiters discovered that the enlistees were not coming through the doors, they panicked. They were unaccustomed and untrained to find the type of young men we needed. The mood of the nation was such that the military was not held in high esteem. Our part in the Vietnam War was just about over, and the reputation of the military had taken some serious hits. As a result, the recruiters enlisted many low-quality recruits and sent them to the depots.

It was expected that the DIs could make Marines out of anyone. The abuse of recruits skyrocketed as the DIs were given an unrealistic goal, and the only way that they saw to accomplish it was to use severe methods. The motivation platoon, correctional custody platoon, reading platoon, and numerous other techniques were employed to accomplish the mission. Many of the recruits conformed while in Boot Camp but reverted to their old habits upon graduation. One need only look at what happened in the operating forces during the early and mid '70s to realize the problem. The disciplinary rate reached unheard-of levels. Pride and discipline, the two most important elements developed and instilled in Boot Camp, were lacking and under the existing policy of recruiting, probably impossible to accomplish.

In 1975, the Corps had a new commandant, General Wilson, who decided that we needed a new direction in recruiting. He set a goal of 75 percent high school graduates for the recruiters to enlist. Many thought that it would be impossible to accomplish and did not agree, but Marines generally get behind a program. The high school diploma was viewed as an indicator of success. Perhaps the individual was not smart, but he had stuck with school for whatever reason and had been successful. Statistics showed that high school grads did better than non-high school grads not only in Boot Camp but later also. There are exceptions on both ends of the spectrum, but even today, the hypothesis holds true. While I was the commanding officer at Parris Island, the attrition rate for non-high school grads was twice that of high school grads.

In 1976, Congress held hearings as a result of recruit abuse at both depots. It shook the roots of the Corps, even more than during the McKeown incident twenty years earlier. The hearings were long, and both the Congress and the American people were incensed when they learned what we were doing to their young men in the name of discipline. It must stop! The mood of the nation continued to be antimilitary and that didn't help. The Marines came within a whisker of losing recruit training, and without that, there would not be a Marine Corps for very long.

Generals Wilson and Barrow agreed to certain changes in Boot Camp. There no longer would be any organized training on Sundays, scheduled training would be limited to ten hours a day, two officers would be assigned to each series instead of one, and the recruits would be granted one hour of free time each evening. That was the start of the renaissance.

Today the new recruits arriving at the depots are better than ever. The average recruit is 5'9", weighs 160 pounds, has 12.3 years of school, and has an IQ of 104. He is bigger—the tailors say that; he is cleaner—the barbers say that; his teeth are better—the dentists say that; and he is healthier—the doctors say that. The mood of the nation has changed again and with it the support for the military.

The commanding generals of the two depots are also the heads of recruiting in each of their areas. No longer can the recruiters tell the depots that they send good men and the depots fail them, nor can the depots tell the recruiters that they are not sending good men. They both have the same boss who has a vested interest in both aspects. Each of these generals or their deputies spend much time visiting the recruiting districts in their respective zones to verify the results and encourage the recruiters. The Corps is the only service that does this, and it makes a big difference in the quality of both recruiting and training. The results speak for themselves.

CHAPTER 1

The Beginning

The National Ensign fluttered softly in the breeze, and next to it fluttered the Battle Color of the First Battalion, Second Marines. The men of the battalion stood at ease as the microphone was placed in front of the battalion commander. A change of command is a significant event in a Marine organization because as a unit's color is passed from the old commander to the new commander, it signifies the change of authority and responsibility. This was such an event, and the old commander prepared to say his farewell to the men of his battalion.

I knew this day was approaching, and yet I didn't know how I could possibly express my feelings for the men of this battalion. As I pondered, I recalled a video movie, which appeared on TV within the last several years. The movie told the story of two football players who played for the Chicago Bears. They both were gifted players who came from different backgrounds—one was Brian Piccolo who happened to be white, and the other, Gale Sayers, who happened to be black. They developed a close relationship, which extended to their families. One year, Gale was injured and became quite frustrated with his physical progress, but Brian would not allow him to quit or feel sorry for himself. Finally, through diligence and perseverance, they overcame this obstacle, and the bond of friendship grew. Together they formed a duo, which was difficult to stop on the field. Years later, Brian started to lose weight and strength. Neither he nor the trainer could understand until finally he went to the hospital where he was diagnosed as having cancer.

This time Gale remained at Brian's side and encouraged him to continue the fight. Unfortunately, it was a losing battle as Brian grew weaker and weaker. At the end of the season, Gale was honored at a banquet as the most courageous player in the National Football league. As he accepted the award and clutched it to his chest, he began to speak. He thanked all of those present for this particular honor, and then spoke of Brian and his fight against cancer. It was an emotional talk, and as he concluded, he said that this award may be his now, but that tonight it would belong to Brian. And then with tears in his eyes and a tremor in his voice as he looked at the audience, he said unashamedly, "I love Brian Piccolo and would like you all to love him." Now, much like Gale Sayers at a different time and place, as I look at you, I can say unashamedly, "I love the men of First Battalion, Second Marines."

So said the battalion commander as he spoke to his men for the final time. The passing of the Battle Color next signified the official change of command, and the executive officer gave the command to "pass in review."

As the final notes of the Marines' Hymn faded on the parade field and the last company had passed in review, I was overcome with two emotions—sadness and joy. Sadness because I was leaving as the commanding officer of what I considered the finest battalion in the Corps, and joy because the following day I would depart to assume command of the Recruit Training Regiment at Parris Island, South Carolina. To add to the festivities, I also was promoted to the rank of colonel at the parade.

There had been no time to think of Parris Island and the new command since being informed about a month before of the new assignment.

The battalion was returning from Okinawa after being the first unit from the Second Marine Division to participate in unit deployment to the Far East. Accounts needed to be exchanged, troop lists organized, briefings conducted, and the details for troop leave planned. To add to that, we were scheduled to be the opposing unit for another Marine battalion undergoing its final test before it deployed overseas.

Now, as I left Camp Lejeune and headed south toward Parris Island, my attention could turn to the task at hand. I thought back on my own experiences almost thirty years before when I headed toward the same destination as a new recruit. It would be different now! During the intervening years, the Corps and the country both had grown older and wiser—not to mention myself. I attempted to recall the memories from my subconscious and compare them with the intervening experiences over the years.

Two of the officers and several of the staff NCOs (SNCOs) of the battalion had recently served at Parris Island and told me of their experiences. They spoke about the quality of the officers and DIs along with the attractiveness of the local area. It would be a challenging assignment. I saw the change in the quality of new Marines entering the division during the two years that I had just completed with the second Marine Division; they were better. The excitement built as the miles passed. What will it look like? How many recruits are there? The questions mounted as I continued to move south.

The signs leading to Parris Island left much to be desired, and if I had not received directions, they would have been missed. The sun had set, and as I drove onto the secondary roads, the Spanish moss hanging from the live oaks gave the illusion of driving through a tunnel. Where is a sign? Finally, as I went around one more curve, the front gate loomed in the headlights, and I could see the Marine sentry on duty. After driving over the causeway and aboard the main post, I looked for familiar landmarks, but they were all gone except for Iron Mike—a Marine statue commemorating the sacrifices of Parris Island Graduates in World War I. Progress and the intervening years had taken its toll as all the Quonset huts and most of the white barracks had been replaced with modern brick buildings.

I drove toward officers' country to the quarters of Tom Campbell to spend the weekend. Tom was an old friend who now commanded the First Battalion. We had known each other for years. He had invited me to stay with his family until my quarters were available, but I thought that it would be better only to remain the weekend and then move into the Bachelor Officer Quarters (BOQ). That would give me the freedom to come and go at my leisure and also preclude any signs of favoritism.

Although it was late in the evening when I arrived, Tom was not at home because the officers of the Regiment were holding a mess night (a formal meal) for the departing regimental commander. That gave me the opportunity to relax and catch up with the news from his wife, Nancy. Tom arrived shortly after midnight, and we spoke for hours about the Regiment. He was as I had remembered—witty, animated, and at this particular time, a little tipsy. The evening passed quickly.

The following week was packed full of briefings and tours as I became reacquainted with how we went about the task of making new Marines. Even with that, the time dragged, as I became more anxious to take charge. The officers and drill instructors looked great going about their daily tasks, and that made me all the more eager to get started.

Finally, the day arrived, and again, as I listened to the final strains of the Marines' Hymn, the responsibility of command was mine. There was so much to learn, but the task had an eager participant. A reception was held in the officers' club immediately following the ceremony, which gave my wife, Grace, and me an opportunity to meet both the military on post and the civilians from the town of Beaufort. The importance of that cannot be overstressed—the relationship between the town and the base was important. We would work at keeping that relationship and improving it if possible.

The Recruit Training Regiment is the largest and most diverse regiment in the Corps. My first challenge was to develop a system to rapidly learn as much as possible about the Regiment. Naturally, the men were interested in who I was and how I intended to command the Regiment. The first priority was to tell them face-to-face. I wanted to ensure that they saw me and heard exactly what I had to say.

It was impossible to speak to all the officers and DIs of the Regiment at the same time since there were thousands of recruits to be trained, so I scheduled the talk in two sessions. The first half of the Regiment was assembled in the theater as I entered from the rear. The operations officer, Lieutenant Colonel Sortino, called them to attention as I moved to the front. The theater was full as the officers and men waited to hear what this new commander had to say.

I felt that it was important for them to know why I thought the way that I did, so I took time to describe my background. I stressed the fact that I had been fortunate over the years to have led everything from a squad to an infantry regiment. I had also taught at Officers' Candidate School (OCS), the Basic School (TBS), and Command and Staff College(C&SC). In addition, I had attended all military schools up to the War College, received a master's degree, a post master's degree in counselor guidance, and needed a few more credits for a doctorate. I continued to stress that I had been very fortunate in assignments. Now the difficult part started. What were we going to do?

There were some of the men who had spent several tours on the drill field and had seen numerous commanding officers (COs) come and go. They probably had heard much of what I would say many times. None of it was revolutionary; however, I not only talked but also practiced what I preached. I started by saying, "I do not intend to spend much time in the office. Paperwork can be done at any time, but one can only talk to the troops when they are available. I will allow you to do your job and will not ambush you. We do not need knee-jerk reactions. If there is a slight problem, it does not mean that we will make drastic quick-fix changes, which will hurt in the long term. I do a considerable amount of thinking aloud, and I do not want the Regiment to react to that. If there is anything that I desire to be done, I will say so directly, and it is not necessary for you to attempt to anticipate my thinking aloud.

"To the best of my knowledge, I have never killed a messenger. Let me explain what I mean by that. In the old days when the king or general received bad news, he had the messenger beheaded. We have become much more sophisticated since that time. Now we chew him out, transfer him, or give him a bad fitness report. When that happens, the boss never receives bad news again. His subordinates will not lie to him. They merely won't tell him any bad news in the hopes that it will improve. Unfortunately, bad news never improves with age. I promise you that I will never kill a messenger. Now, on the other side of the coin, I will become very upset if I learn about something that you should have told me. With the quality of the Marines that we have in this regiment, there is absolutely nothing that we cannot fix, and the sooner that we know it, the faster and the quicker that it can be fixed. I know that you have probably heard this before, but trust me. I am absolutely serious.

"We will continue to refine training, and if there is a better way, we will try it. With that in mind, let's talk about the standing operating procedure (SOP). That document was written by Marines just like you and me about how to train recruits. We will obey it, but if there is any aspect of it that prevents us from doing the very best job, we will get it changed. If our rationale is correct, headquarters will support us.

"Another topic is integrity. Your conduct must be beyond reproach. You must not only do what is correct, but it also must appear correct. If everyone thinks that you are a liar, then you may as well be one. Let me give you an example of what I mean. In 1979-80, I was assigned to an unaccompanied tour in Korea. For the entire year, I went to great lengths to ensure that I never placed myself in a compromising position such that someone could possibly think that I was being unfaithful to my wife. I shared a house with a navy lieutenant commander, and we had a maid that did the housework and laundry. The last week of my tour, the maid asked if I could go to the gate and escort her daughter onto the post. Her daughter did not have an ID card, and the sentry would not allow her aboard without an escort. I thought nothing of it and went to the gate, where I met a very attractive young lady of about seventeen. As we came on post and walked toward my quarters, we met a Marine captain who gave me a salute and a cheery 'Good morning, sir.' It was approximately 8:00 am, and here was a lieutenant colonel with a very attractive young lady obviously heading toward his quarters. There was nothing that I could say to retrieve the situation, and I could see one year go down the tubes. That's what I mean by perception." The audience laughed because they too knew what was going through the captain's mind. I covered a couple of other items and then opened it up to questions.

Questions were then asked from the audience, and after a short period, the meeting ended. At least they had heard what I had to say, and now they could judge me by my actions. It was obvious from the innocuous questions that they would need more than words before they fully believed what they had heard.

First Impressions

I have always believed that the morale of a unit starts at breakfast in the mess hall. As a result, I had made it a habit over the years to always check the mess hall to insure that it ran like McDonalds—clean, fast, nutritious, and tasty. All four battalions in the Regiment operated their own mess halls, and each mess could seat about one thousand recruits at a time. They allowed ten minutes to go through the line per series, followed by twenty minutes to eat. The recruit series moved through the mess hall in an unending procession. The ability to feed so many in such a short period of time was a tribute to the cooks and DIs.

I entered the Second Battalion mess from the scullery near the parking lot. The recruits on mess duty sounded off with a loud "Good morning, sir" as the cooks looked up from their tasks to see who had entered their domain. I looked around there, checked the serving line, and then proceeded to the recruit seating area. I spoke to several of the recruits and asked questions in order to get their impressions of Boot Camp.

The *stomp, stomp, stomp* of boots echoed in the building as new platoons continued to arrive. "Ready step, left face, forward march," sounded as the recruit-in-charge issued orders to the platoon to move through the line. All eyes were fixed to the front as they rapidly moved under the watchful eyes of the ever-present DIs.

It was obvious that the recruits were uneasy as I passed among the tables and spoke with many of them. *Who is this colonel who seems to be interested in the chow and treatment? Why is he here among us?* One could almost hear the questions going through their minds. I stopped at a table and asked, "How's the chow?" It was the same everywhere. They immediately dropped their forks, sat at attention, and responded, "Fine, sir." "Is it hot?" "Yes, sir." Each time, I would tell them to relax and look at me and then spend a moment or two asking where they were from and why they had joined the Corps.

As I continued, I could sense that someone was watching me. The permanent personnel ate in a separate section of the mess, and it was normally full of officers, DIs, and other Marines assigned to the regiment. Now was no exception and they were keenly aware of my presence as though I were an outsider intruding into their territory. *Look, the colonel is in the mess talking to recruits,* one could almost hear them thinking. And then it immediately dawned on them. *The recruits are talking to the colonel. What are they telling him?* There couldn't have been a bigger impact if I had dropped a grenade.

After a short interval, I moved into the permanent personnel section and spoke to several of the DIs. They too were uneasy, much like the recruits. "How long have you been on the field, Sergeant?" A tall, neat-looking drill instructor responded, "One year, sir." "How do you like it?" I asked. He went on to give me his opinion of the recruits and the training but remained rather reserved. Better to wait and see what this new colonel wanted to hear. The other DIs watched as we chatted and probably felt relieved that it was not they who had been selected. I remained in the mess for a while longer to ensure that they knew I was interested, and then left.

Later that same day, I had the driver take me to Page Field, which is an abandoned WWII airfield that is used to conduct all the field training. Since it has been unused as an airfield for decades, many of the grassy areas off the runways had been planted with pine trees, which made it quite suitable for small unit tactics. At this particular juncture, the recruits spent five days in the field learning the basic field skills such as fire team and squad tactics, mines and booby traps, hiking, the infiltration course, combat firing, and numerous other techniques. The recruit series, number 1024, was the present occupant, and it ran everywhere it went. There never seemed to be enough time.

Page Field had several bivouac sites to accommodate the various series during their training evolutions, and the DIs and officers remained with them throughout the field training. It looked good, and the men appeared to be enthusiastic. Now I could see firsthand what we did to prepare these men for the Fleet Marine Forces. It was not complicated or detailed, but it was obvious that a lot of material was crammed into a short period of time. *Take notes and just watch,* I reminded myself.

The remainder of that first day is a blur. The time flew, and before I realized, it ended as I went to my quarters and then ran four miles. The heat, even in the evening, was stifling. *That's one thing that hasn't changed,* I thought.

I planned to watch a pickup the following morning. When the recruits arrive, they spend the first three or four days in the receiving barracks where they undergo testing, inoculations, issue of clothing, and other administrative matters. During that time, they are introduced to the military in a low-stress mode.

When that is complete, they are taken to their assigned battalion at 0600 in the morning. All their newly issued clothing goes with them, and they are formed in their squad bay to await the drill instructor. That is the mythical man that they have heard so much about.

Fortunately, my family remained in North Carolina so that my children could finish school; therefore I could come and go as I pleased. Early mornings or late evenings made no difference. I arrived at the designated barracks at 0600. The squad bay was immaculate. Everything was lined up, and there were signs with specific messages on all the bulkheads: left-port, right-starboard, ceiling-overhead, floor-deck, wall-bulkhead, toilet-head, general orders, leadership traits, and famous sayings. Even the head had signs on all the bulkheads so that the recruits would be constantly faced with information.

Six or eight rows of recruits were formed facing the front as the receiving sergeant explained what was about to happen. "Seats, now when I give you the word, you will sit at attention as the battalion commander enters. He will explain what will happen next. You are in platoon 2036 and series 2036, Second Battalion." He went on to describe other details, which were totally lost because they had only one thing on their mind—who was the drill instructor?

Presently, he sounded off, "Pla-toon, a-ten-hut." From their front, through a door, came a lieutenant colonel (Lt. Col.) and a sergeant major (Sgt. Maj.). They marched, flanked, and halted in front of the startled recruits. "My name is Lieutenant Colonel Moore, and I am your battalion commander. The man on my left is Sergeant Major Fish. He advises me on all matters concerning the enlisted men in this battalion." He went on to explain what was expected of them to successfully complete recruit training and then abruptly introduced two more men who appeared to their front—the company commander and first sergeant. Now the company commander spoke and then introduced the two series officers and the series chief drill instructor. Finally, the drill instructors were in front of the platoon. The senior DI stood well over six feet with broad shoulders narrowed to a slim waist. His brass and shoes glistened like diamonds. He was impressive! They eyed each other as the senior drill instructor spoke, "My name is Staff Sergeant (SSgt) McGhee, and I am your senior drill instructor. Along with Sergeant Jones and Sergeant Burns, our mission is to train each one of you to become a Marine. A Marine is characterized as one who possesses the highest in military virtue. He obeys orders, respects his seniors, and strives constantly to be the best in everything he does. Discipline and spirit are the hallmark of a Marine, and these qualities are the goals of your training here. Every recruit here, whether you are fat or skinny, tall or short, fast or slow, can become a Marine if you can develop self-discipline and spirit. We will make every effort to train you, even after some of you have given up on yourselves. Starting now, you will treat me and other Marines with the highest respect, and you will obey all orders without question. We have earned our place as Marines, and we will accept nothing less than that from you. I will treat you just as I do my fellow Marines, with firmness, fairness, dignity, and compassion. As such, I am not going to threaten you with physical harm, abuse you, or harass you, nor will I tolerate such behavior from anyone else, Marine or recruit. If anyone should abuse or mistreat you, I will expect you to report such incidents to me. Further, if you believe that I have mistreated you, I expect you to report it to the series commander, Lieutenant Ouzts. My drill instructors will be with you every day, everywhere you go. I have told you what my drill instructors and I will do.

"For your part, we will expect you to give 100 percent of yourself at all times. Now this is specifically what we expect you to do:

a. You must do everything you are told to do, quickly and willingly.
b. You will treat all Marines and recruits with courtesy and respect.
c. You must be completely honest in everything you do. A Marine never lies, cheats, or compromises.

d. You must respect the rights and property of all other persons. A Marine never steals.
e. You must be proud of yourself and the uniform you wear.
f. You must try your best to learn the things you will be taught. Everything we teach you is important and must be remembered.
g. You must work hard to strengthen your body.
h. Above all else, you must never quit or give up. We cannot train you and help you unless you want to become a Marine—unless you are willing to give your very best! We offer you the challenge of recruit training—the opportunity to earn the right to be a United States Marine!"

Staff sergeant McGhee had not stood still as he spoke to his new platoon but, rather, moved from side to side and looked most of the recruits in the eyes. One could sense that they knew he would accept nothing less than the very best. There was no doubt in their minds that he was deadly serious. As he finished, the series officer stepped in front of the three DIs and told them to raise their right hands to retake the DI Pledge. "These recruits are entrusted to my care. I will train them to the best of my ability. I will develop them into smartly disciplined, physically fit, basically trained Marines, thoroughly indoctrinated in love of Corps and country. I will demand of them and demonstrate by my own example the highest standards of personal conduct, morality, and professional skill."

This pledge is first taken by each DI as he successfully completes DI school and retaken before the start of training for each platoon. The lieutenant left the squad bay, and Staff Sergeant McGhee told his DIs, "Make Marines of these recruits."

Now all hell broke loose as the DIs started to shout orders to the recruits in the typical DI fashion. The time had come; the honeymoon was over. The recruits responded as well as they could, but most of them had no idea what was being said. They would learn!

This routine was standard for all new series, and each of the talks by the DIs was a prepared speech so that nothing was left to chance. I remained for only a few minutes and then left to visit other parts of the Regiment. Later that morning, I attended my first commanding general conference. It was rather productive, and I was greatly relieved. My experience had been that when meetings were held on a routine basis, they usually evolved into a waste of time. Most of the staff do not want to appear nonproductive, so its members dream up various items to bring to the attention of the boss. In my view, meetings are best held when there is something to settle or plans to prepare. When there are definite goals in mind, they are normally much more productive. That will work, but only if the staff is constantly coordinating with other elements, both higher and lower. Meetings should be agenda-driven and time-constrained. The commanding officer (CO) can overcome the lack of meetings by constantly moving around and determining that his orders are being carried out but, more importantly, that the *intent* of his orders are fully understood.

One or two examples will make that point quite clear. At Parris Island, the heat in the summer is legendary. In order to avoid harming the recruits and permanent personnel, there is a very detailed routine and procedure to reduce heat casualties. In addition to other procedures, showers are installed on all the athletic fields, and each time a unit passes during its run, it goes through the showers to cool off. It has been very effective in eliminating heat casualties.

One day in the early fall, while we were still on the summer routine, it was cold and windy. In fact, a sweat suit for running would not have been uncomfortable. As I approached one of the fields, I could see a series running through the showers. I ran up next to the lieutenant and asked why he was going through the showers on such a cold day. As we ran along, he explained that the regulations stated that during HOTSOP, you must run the recruits through the showers. In his mind, he was only following orders, and it was not necessary to make a judgment call if the circumstances had changed. An officer is paid and truly earns respect and trust by thinking. As we ran, I explained this to the young officer. The purpose of the regulations was to assist and guide, but they could never replace thinking. We have the showers to cool the bodies off, but common sense should dictate that if it is cold, then it is not necessary to use them and you may cause hypothermia. That was a case of blind obedience.

I also found the opposite during COLDSOP when the weather was uncommonly hot. In that particular case, the recruits were running in sweat gear with no showers when they could have been in shorts and shirt. Naturally, I had another conversation with a lieutenant about utilizing initiative and judgment. It seemed that they were reluctant to use initiative and possibly make a mistake rather than blindly follow orders.

That is a tendency that can develop when subordinates in units are not encouraged to use their initiative and to *think.*

As the days extended into weeks, I became more comfortable with the Regiment, but I was not sure that the feeling was mutual. After spending the last two years with the Second Marine Division, I was accustomed to the officers and men speaking their mind. That was not completely true here. When I asked an open-ended question, I would receive a yes or no answer. The officers and men would not talk freely. It was as though I was an outsider or spy. If I intended to get them to assist, then they had to be convinced that I was not the enemy. Talking was not the sole answer. It would occur when they realized that my actions were in direct line with my words and we were all in the same boat and must pull on the oars together. The first move was to open the lines of communications with the DIs. I informed the battalion commanders that I intended to talk to a DI from each of the companies every Friday. I wanted to use that as a vehicle to pick the DIs' brains and also allow them to pick mine. I wanted the commander's help to put it across and asked them what they thought of the idea. It did not meet with unanimous approval because they were afraid that I would learn about things before they did and that they would look bad. They were afraid that they would be ambushed. I could understand their fears, but they would need to learn that I was absolutely serious about opening the lines of communications and not concerned about discovering trivia before they did.

The meetings were implemented and continued each Friday until my transfer over two years later. At times, these discussions lasted up to four hours with some of the groups being very lively and others being difficult to get started.

After a while, I expanded it and also had talks with the first sergeants and sergeant majors and, at other times, the company grade officers.

At any rate, they had the desired result because many of the real and perceived problems of the DIs were corrected. They came to realize that the command was truly interested in their welfare and would go to extremes to make conditions better. During most of the talks in the first year, I spoke the initial forty-five minutes about history and how we arrived at where we were and where we were going in recruit training. It started something like this: "In my last command, I would get together with eight or ten troops each week and check to see what kind of word they were getting as compared to the word that had been passed. The difference initially was amazing. As an example, if I would take the eight of you and whisper something into the first man's ear and he, in turn, did the same, by the time it arrived at the last man, it would be different. That is the filter working and how the word becomes garbled. We can live with that, but what we cannot live with is if the word is completely different. Unfortunately, that occurs at times, but hopefully these discussions will help to reduce that. I do not intend to go to your battalion commanders after these discussions and tell them who said what. Conversely, I will not make any decisions here and blindside the commanders. When there is something to be changed, it will be passed through the chain of command. In addition, this will give me an opportunity to pick your brains and for you to pick mine. In both cases we will become better informed.

"You drill instructors are among the finest NCOs in the Corps. To become a DI, one must first have a superb record, then be screened, and finally, trained at the DI School. At the DI School, you were given all the necessary tools to become a superb DI, but in the process, we had about 35 percent attrition.

"Just as everyone cannot be a Marine, so it is that every Marine cannot be a DI. Even after all this screening and training, we have about 10 percent of our DIs commit suicide each year—professional suicide. They are relieved for cause! They are relieved for violating orders. When a Marine is relieved for cause, he is through in the Corps. With very few exceptions, when the time comes to reenlist, he will not be recommended.

"Why is it that this magnificent Marine deliberately, over prolonged periods of time, disobeys orders? This same Marine would never even consider doing it any place else except here, and he does it for one major reason—to make a Marine. He does it because that is what was done to him, or he believes that it was, and he became a superb Marine. Naturally he believes that is what made him so good. Nothing could be further from the truth. He became good because of all the good things that his DI and every other leader taught him, and in spite of the garbage. I have spoken to over one hundred DIs [this figure changed throughout my tour and eventually ended up as nine hundred] and have found only three [this also changed to a total of seven] who either were not victims of or did not see abuse when they were in Boot Camp. It depended on when they came through exactly what happened, but it was abuse nonetheless. What I am saying is that almost all of them were exposed to some poor examples and became good Marines in spite of it. That is critical because it coincides with other types of behaviors, which have been studied for years. Alcoholics generally come from families of alcoholics. The father, mother, brother, aunt, uncle, etc., had a drinking problem. That was the role model, and unfortunately, many from that environment follow suit. Another example is child abusers—sixty to seventy percent of child abusers themselves were abused as children. These are not my figures but, rather, the countless studies conducted over the years.

"One would suspect that after suffering all the heartache and pain from such behaviors that the victims would be the last to do it. Unfortunately, that is not true—they are the first. If that is true, then it makes sense to me that our DIs who have either witnessed or been victims of some type of abuse could very easily follow suit.

"If the punishment were ten years in the brig and a dishonorable discharge for abusing a recruit, nothing would change because those who do it believe that it must be done to make a Marine, and they do not intend to be caught. It's like a bank robber. If it were absolutely certain that every bank robber was captured as he exited the bank, then there would be no bank robbers. If it were guaranteed that everyone who had a drink and got behind the wheel of an auto dropped dead, then drunk driving would cease. Everyone believes that it is always the other guy who will have those problems.

"We all know that neither of these things will happen, and so they continue. The same is true in recruit training—it will always be the other guy. The only way that this will change in Boot Camp is to change attitudes. We already change the attitudes of twenty-five thousand men each year, the recruits. Now I wish to add six hundred more, the DIs. When that happens—you notice I said *when*, not *if*, because it is going to happen—then it will be the most significant change that has ever occurred in Boot Camp.

"It must happen because the future of our Corps is at stake. In 1956, when six recruits died in Ribbon Creek, it was not intentional. Sergeant McKeown did not hold their heads underwater.

"He did not intend to have six recruits die, but they did. In 1975, we did not intend to beat Private McClure to death with a pugil stick, but we did.

"The Marine Corps came within an absolute whisker of losing recruit training following the congressional hearings in 1976. The American people and Congress were livid when they discovered what we were doing to their young men in the name of discipline. I have copies of speeches from the commanding general given to the officers and DIs at Parris Island at that time, and you can sense the panic. We were terrified that we would lose Boot Camp. You may think that it could never be done, but don't you believe it. We already have the Defense Logistics Agency, the Defense Communications Agency, and the Defense Intelligence Agency. We would have the Defense Recruit Training Command. It would be eight weeks long and conducted at such places as San Diego, Fort Dix, the Great Lakes, and Fort Jackson. There would be army troop handlers, navy troop handlers, air force troop handlers, and Marine troop handlers. At the end of basic training, our Marines, many of whom would not be trained by a DI, would go to all the same places as they do now. The Marine Corps that we now know would cease to exist in about four years because the two most important things that we try to instill and develop in Boot Camp, pride and discipline, could not be done. We must have Boot Camp! That is what is at stake any time a DI violates his orders. I doubt that there is a DI here who would intentionally harm a recruit, however, it is not what one intends to do but what actually happens.

The sad part is that it need not be done. Brutality does not make a Marine. It never has and it never will. It does not occur in the operating forces. The troops will not tolerate it. They will fight back. It is only a recruit who will not fight back.

I am not going to sit here and say that we have never had, and perhaps do not now have, heavy-handed NCOs in the fleet, but the troops will fight back by doing something.

"The benefit of this is that the DI will leave Parris Island with his hat in his hand, and he will be a better NCO. He will be better, and the Corps will be better. The final point is the recruits. When they return in five or ten years, as drill instructors, they will train their recruits as they were trained. The recruit abuse monster will be dead once and for all. Does this all make sense to you guys? Do you see what is at stake?"

The reaction generally was the same. I felt that this was probably the only time that many of them heard a full explanation of recruit training, and they really did not know how to respond. They would hear this time after time from now on until they realized how important that it was.

After the pregnant pause, I would continue, "Now I want to hear what you have to say. Let me first preface that by saying that my intent is to produce the very best basic Marine that we can possibly produce and save drill instructors. If you were sitting in my seat and could change one thing in the Regiment, what would you change? If it means changing regulations that will accomplish those two missions, then we will do that."

Normally the discussions would continue for up to three more hours, and the number of suggestions and resulting changes were many. There were times when it would be after 1800 and we were still at it. The DIs gave these discussions a name, the "fireside chat with the colonel."

The Generals

About three weeks after assuming command of the Regiment, the new commanding general (CG) reported aboard, Major General J. J. McMonagle. He and I had served together several times, and we knew how each other thought. He had just completed two years as the deputy commanding general at the other recruit depot in San Diego. Naturally there was a depot size change of command ceremony with two regiments in review. It was a golden opportunity to view about half of the Regiment on parade along with many of the officers and staff NCOs. There were several rehearsals preceding the ceremony with one day being hotter than the next. The ever-present sand flea received his invitation to both the rehearsals and ceremony and brought his family and friends. Ask any Marine who has ever been to Parris Island, and he will be able to tell a few stories about the sand fleas. They absolutely love to flock around Marines, and their appetites are insatiable. Parris Island would not be the same without these insects of flying teeth.

As the summer wore on and the days became hotter, we received a visit by the commandant, General Robert H. Barrow. My battalion had been attached to his regiment in Vietnam during Operation Dewey Canyon in 1969. Without doubt, he was the leading expert on recruit training. He had been at the headquarters during the congressional hearings in 1976 and had been called upon to testify. He also had been a recruit, a DI, and the commanding general of Parris Island. He definitely had the background and insight into how to make a Marine.

One of the great advantages of a visit by a group or an important person to Parris Island was that they saw exactly what we were doing. There were no special shows to impress them.

We simply allowed them to see exactly what was taking place on that particular day. Since there were always plenty of recruits in training throughout the island doing many different things, that was not a problem. For the commandant, we did just that.

As it turned out, he could not have picked a better day because we had recruits in all phases of training doing everything. There was a colors ceremony, gas chamber, command inspection, rifle range, classroom instruction, final drill, PT, swimming, pugil sticks, and combat firing.

The CG asked me to ride in the sedan with him and the commandant. That was a real education, and I picked up some pointers, which I would use later. General Barrow enjoyed Parris Island and seemed to know all its nooks and crannies.

At the combat firing range, he spoke with many of the recruits. To the rear of each firing point, there was a sign with printed safety regulations and a description of what the recruits were expected to do. He randomly selected various recruits and asked them to read the sign for him since he had forgotten his glasses. He remembered the days from the early '70s when we had less than 50 percent high school graduates and it was necessary to teach many of them how to read and write. We no longer had those problems, and he was merely checking it out. To the DIs and the other permanent personnel he asked, "How are these new recruits?" Almost without exception, he was pleased with what he heard. He deserved to be pleased because he was one of the driving forces behind the rise in quality of the men that we now recruited. It had been his idea to combine the recruiting command and recruit training command under one head so that the quality could be better controlled. It worked!

At the swimming pool and gas chamber, he continued to eyeball the recruits and question the DIs. It was obvious that he was pleased with what he saw and did not see. He turned to First Sergeant Moore, the first sergeant of F Company. He had worked for the general as a DI in the early '70s. He said, "Look at them, you can see the quality. After more than thirty years, one has a gut feeling about men. First Sergeant, do you remember when many of the recruits that we had did not look this good? We had a lot of fat bodies. They even looked sneaky." The first sergeant, who was not known to be a man of few words but was totally respected throughout the Regiment, smiled and responded, "General, they were sneaky."

Back at mainside, the general spent almost an hour inspecting a platoon, which was undergoing its final inspection before graduation. He spoke to nearly every recruit and asked questions about his home or family. One recruit responded that he came from Louisville, Kentucky. The commandant looked at the recruit and said that the Louisville Sluggers are made there. Without any hesitation, the recruit responded, "No, sir," and then went on to explain where they were made. The recruit's DI almost had a heart attack listening to one of his recruits correcting the commandant.

After the inspection, he went to the front of the platoon and explained that even the commandant could learn from a recruit and told the story about the Louisville Sluggers. He then asked for a show of hands of all those men who had relatives who had served in the Corps. About half of the platoon raised their hands. "We grow our own," he smiled.

Throughout the day he expounded on the importance of Boot Camp and the necessity of training Marines in a challenging, fair, and dignified manner.

I listened and took many mental notes because much of it would be applied later. I cannot say how much that the commandant learned on the visit, but I picked up numerous gems of wisdom.

His final stop before departing was the DI school, where he spoke to the students. He told them how important that it was to have Boot Camp. "We are professionals, and as professionals we are accountable for our actions. I will tell you the secret to being a successful DI, and it must be a secret because no one knows. The one person whom you think that you have the most control over and whom you can dictate to is the same person who will do you in—the recruit. He must respond, but he still writes home, and he can write to his congressman if he desires. You don't have as much control as you think. Again, as a professional, you are accountable for your actions." He shared a few stories from his background, and then he was gone.

The commandant had given me many ideas about the types of questions to ask. I made a few mental adjustments about the types of questions to ask and charged ahead. It is amazing what one can learn if only he asks the proper questions.

All the recruits are volunteers, and they could have joined any of the services. In the past, many of our career Marines joined in order to avoid the draft and discovered that the Corps was their cup of tea. After listening to General Barrow, I started asking the recruits, "How many of you went to see the recruiter without his ever getting in touch with you in any way shape or form?" More than half indicated that they had gone to see the recruiter. When I asked why, there were many responses.

Relatives in the Corps were a big one, but another one was the challenge or direction, which they were hoping to find. They were looking for something, and many could not say what, but they hoped to find it in the Corps. A surprising answer was that they had spoken to a Marine who had recently graduated from Boot Camp.

I also asked if Boot Camp was what they thought it would be. Many of them responded no, and when asked why, they could not really provide an answer. The greatest percentage of these had relatives who had gone through the training and told them about it. Additional questioning revealed that they expected to see what one must classify as abuse. "Why would you join if you thought that you would be beaten?" The answer almost always was that they thought that was what it took to make a man tough. That also contributed to the unending problem of changing attitudes.

Many of their fathers or uncles had gone through Boot Camp about the same period that I had. I shared my observations with them and the DIs. "I went through Boot Camp in 1953, and I can assure you that Boot Camp today is at least twice as tough as it was when I went through. You must do more than I did, and the supervision is much closer. In those days, there was no standard PT program. PT was whatever the DI wanted it to be, and more often than not, that meant running in place and duck walking. There was no PT test as there is now. We were in shape, but not as good as you are going to be."

I am sure that many of them did not believe me or thought that I merely said that in order to justify the present system. Contrary to that, I firmly believe it.

CHAPTER 2

Why Abuse

The stories about recruit training are well-known, and whenever current Marines or old Marines gather, they compare who had it rougher in Boot Camp. Some of it is imagination, but unfortunately, much of it is true. After talking to a great number of Marines who went through Boot Camp as far back as the '30s, I have arrived at the following opinions. I cannot prove all of this, but it does make sense. I believe that systematic abuse started in about 1949 or 1950. Prior to that time, I'm sure that there were some DIs who were heavy-handed, but it was not institutionalized. During World War II, we had a mission to prepare men to fight, and there was little time to dream up ways to harass the troops. It was almost a crusade, and we were the crusaders going off to destroy the infidels.

After winning the war, the DIs sat around and told stories about how hard it was and what they had been through both in Boot Camp and since. They had a chest full of ribbons to back them up, and as the years passed, an ever-increasing group of new DIs with no combat experience wearied of listening to how hard it was in the old days. They had not been old enough to have served and they could not join in the talks. They thought to themselves, *If only I had been old enough, I too would be wearing a chest full of ribbons and be hard, and to prove it, I'll produce harder Marines than the old salts.* Then it started! They decided that they would produce the hardest Marines ever. They required their recruits to do things well beyond what the regulations and the old salts did. The illegality and unfairness of their actions did not matter because they had a point to prove both to themselves and the older Marines.

Shortly after this, the Korean War started, and the Corps went from a demobilized force to a much larger one. The junior DI in a platoon would be told to select two of his recruits to become the junior DIs for his next platoon as he became the senior. Naturally these new Marines knew nothing about the Corps except Boot Camp. They became DIs, and the better ones were promoted rather rapidly. In time, they too were told to select two of their recruits to become junior DIs for them. About this time the wounded and veterans from the Korean War started returning to be DIs, and the cycle accelerated. The recruits needed to be prepared for war! They had to be "combat Marines" even though that was not the mission.

There are many exceptions to this theory because numerous new DIs performed magnificently. However, it does answer the question about why we did have some serious problems. Why else would a DI state at his court martial, after having been convicted of beating his recruits, "You do not understand, that is what you must do to make a Marine"?

To reinforce this explanation, there have been numerous books written on the topic of recruit training. *To Keep Our Honor Clean* addresses Boot Camp in 1951, and although it is fiction, it is based on fact written by an old Marine who is now a writer in New York. The main characters consisted of a career staff sergeant as the senior DI, a sadistic sergeant as the experienced junior, and a corporal as the new DI who was serving a tour prior to attending officer candidate school. After reading that book, I wrote to that particular individual and explained how we now trained our recruits and invited him to visit Boot Camp at Parris Island. He never responded.

I had forgotten most of the situations described in that book, but it triggered my memory, and I recalled seeing almost everything that was described. In those days, it was a capital crime to break ranks—that meant moving through a platoon or between a platoon and its DI. If that happened, the platoon literally beat the shit out of the offender.

Some DIs would position themselves so that an unsuspecting recruit would unintentionally walk between him and his platoon. They took sadistic pleasure in what followed. The competition among the platoons was absolutely cutthroat. Winning at any cost seemed to be the goal. As I read the book, I vowed to ensure that we would not return to that type of behavior. We could not afford it.

During the congressional hearings in 1976 following the death of a recruit at San Diego and the shooting of another recruit at Parris Island, a survey of personnel at Parris Island was conducted. The questionnaire was answered by 243 Marines: 46 or 19 percent were DI students, 119 or 49 percent were DIs on the field with less than six months' experience; 64 or 26 percent were DIs with more than six months experience; and the remaining 6 percent were non-DI supervisory personnel.

About two thirds of the respondents felt that an effective DI had the following characteristics:

Unfriendly—79.5%	Tough—61.1%
Cold—62.8%	Strong—3.7%
Tense—60.8%	Kind—71.6%
Profane—78.1%	Forceful—67.7%
Easy—87.7%	

Over half also thought that the ideal DI was impatient (52.4 percent) and loud (55.0 percent).

The respondents' responses to what characteristics were possessed by the average recruit also were interesting. About two thirds believed the average recruit was as follows:

Unmotivated—94.3%	Insincere—76.4%
Lazy—82.7%	Liar—65.7%
Good—72.2%	Soft—79.2%
Awkward—63.0%	Ignorant—74.7%

They were less certain that he was as follows:

Disciplined—49.4%	Clean—51.0%
Mature—51.3%	Ugly—56.5%
Responsible—51.1%	

The questionnaire recorded the following opinions of the majority:

a. Over 95 percent agreed, 74 percent strongly, that a DI should have more leeway in disciplining recruits.
b. Over 95 percent agreed, 69 percent strongly, that a DI should use fear in teaching discipline.
c. Over 95 percent disagreed, 60 percent strongly, that there is good reason for almost all recruit training regulations restricting what DIs may or may not do.
d. Over 90 percent agreed, 69 percent strongly, that there should be less officer supervision of DIs.

e. Over 90 percent agreed that a DI is justified in maltreating recruits on occasion; 45 percent strongly agreed.
f. Over 87 percent agreed, 53 percent strongly, that DIs should be able to accept a graduation gift from their platoon.
g. Over 77 percent agreed that recruits should be allowed to shine DIs' shoes and brass.

Is it any wonder that we had a problem? If one has no respect for individuals, then it normally follows that the treatment is less than appropriate. That holds true in any environment whether it is a school or a business or, in this case, Boot Camp. The major goal must be to change attitudes through reason, example, persistence, and training. In the past we had, more often than not, treated the symptom rather than the cause. We added more regulations, more supervision, and more punishment. That is the typical answer most organizations attempt when confronted with a difficult problem, and yet it is not the total answer.

Those opinions cited are not entirely dead as reflected in a letter that a DI wrote to Senator Glenn in 1983. He had graduated from Boot Camp in 1978 and reported to the drill field in 1982. It was a lengthy letter in which he challenged many of the programs for making Marines. We already had made numerous adjustments to recruit training, and in his letter he explained, among other things, why he felt that recruits should be led by fear. In one section, he bemoaned the alleviation of *excessive* stress at the initial receiving point at Parris Island and what he considered to be the result for the DI:

"This creates difficulties for us when the recruits are delivered to the drill instructors who are going to take them through training. The recruits are not as scared as they should be because the culture shock has worn off. So the DI has to work all the harder to reestablish that fear and to make it grow to the necessary proportions. This fear is a very vital part of recruit training. A drill instructor has got to rule his platoon with a dictatorial hand.

He has got to rule by fear. The recruits do as he orders because they think that he is crazy. They are afraid of him. They are afraid of what he is going to do to them. They are afraid of the punishment he is going to inflict on them if they do not obey him. A drill instructor cannot lead his platoon by encouragement or by showing them the way and still expect them to follow. Most recruits are not anywhere mature enough to realize that what the DI is doing to him is for his own benefit. Even if they have heard the old story, "No pain, no gain," they are often not willing to take it to the necessary limits. Many of them are street punks who have never had any respect for authority in their lives. They are used to taking switchblades with them to school. They are used to telling their teachers to go to hell. They tell their parents to go suck on an egg. They call a policeman a filthy pig. The only way they are going to make the transition to a highly disciplined Marine is if the drill instructor leads by fear. This is especially vital in the first half of training. Some recruits can be lead by less fear later on because they begin to mature. Only later do they realize that what we expect of them is for *their* own benefit, and not for the feeding of any illusions of personal grandeur that I might have."

Those are the thoughts of a DI about the recruits in 1983, and they are out of step with reality. They were false perceptions and received a great amount of attention in an effort to change them. More orders or more supervision would not do it. One must remember that this is a Marine who went through Boot Camp in 1978 and had only four years in the Corps. I knew who this Marine was and could very easily have had him transferred, but I decided to try and change his opinion. If I could not win these small battles, then there was no hope for the long-range goals.

Although an individual could attend the college of his choice if he had the grades and the money, he could not enlist in the Corps if he had a police record or a drug problem. Less than 80 percent of our young completed high school, and we were recruiting 97 percent high school graduates. In effect, we were much better than society as a whole.

Lieutenant General Krulak, USMC (Ret), said it best in his article in the April 1982 issue of the *Marine Corps Gazette* when he summarized traditional DI philosophy in these words: "In two and a half months, I have to turn these *seventy* individuals into a team of obedient Marines who believe in their buddies and the Corps, who can survive on the battlefield—and my superiors want no excuses. The recruits are young and often ignorant. Many of them have never been part of anything meaningful; many have never been motivated to do anything useful. Some of them are physically weak. Some of them have never had to respond to authority and do not know the meaning of obedience. And I know how to do it. The captains and colonels don't know how. Very few of them have ever been through it. I have, and I intend to do what is needed so that the recruits will end up as useful members of a team—a credit to me, the Corps, and their country."

I am sure that there continue to be Marines who honestly believe this. It is up to the leadership to convince them otherwise. The final description should convince readers why we had, and at times continue to have, problems in Boot Camp. This was a letter written by a Marine to the commandant in February 1983 who went through Boot Camp in 1969.

Dear Commandant,

I don't know why I didn't think to write this to you sooner. The chain of command makes no difference now and at last I feel relatively safe from your reach.

I suppose you must know these things but maybe if I write them one more time I can be rid of the memories and nightmares, and maybe the bitterness won't burn in my gut. No, I was never in Vietnam, or I suspect would be even worse. The memories I have are from Boot Camp in 1969.

I was one of eighty young men who formed platoon 3148 on 4 Aug. 69, in San Diego. I was in good physical shape in the beginning, my hair was shorter than most, and I had a capable intellect. I believed in the cause of Vietnam then and I believed in the rightness of my government. I believed in many things I didn't understand then.

The first night in Boot Camp, after the haircuts, the clothes issue, and the showers, we were run up and down the roads and through the sandlots of MCRD. For most of the time we were forced to hold our filled duffel bags above our heads, and the name-calling and shouting started. So did the slaps, the punches, and the kicks. In the early morning dark we stopped before a blackboard and we were told to write home to tell our families we had arrived safely and to send our address, but in the few minutes we were given few of us could find the writing materials we had been issued and it was too dark to read the address on the blackboard. The letters were nothing but folded pieces of paper saying nothing, addressed to no one.

In the August heat we not allowed to stop that night, or anytime in the next few weeks, to get a drink, except on those occasional trips to the head where those who could not get to the sinks hurried to the urinals and toilets for a few handfuls of water. On the third day as we were learning to do "about face" I unknowingly turned to the left instead of the right. The DI called me over, propped his foot on the raised platform between us, grabbed me by the collars of my shirt, and drove my chest into his knee. Then after a few slaps and a few names he told me what I was doing wrong.

As platoon secretary for a time I filled out daily reports of the status of the recruits in the platoon. There were five who were given medical discharges in the first few weeks. They were all young men who were driven further than they could stand and were sent home to their families insane. Other reports during the twelve weeks frequently reported recruits had fallen out of bed at night and broken arms and legs, and seriously damaged internal organs when in fact these injuries were the result of the beatings by the DIs and sometimes even by squad leaders the DIs appointed.

Squad leaders were often held responsible for the actions of their squads and brutally beaten for someone's misstep on the parade field. Often the beatings and harassment had nothing to do with any misdeeds but were used to fill time between scheduled events. One morning, during one of my tenures as a squad leader, we were inadvertently called out to go to class too early. The DIs entered the closest Quonset hut and started tearing the beds apart. I was called in and ordered to my "knuckles," the pushup position with closed fist, and the DI caught my chest with the crook of his boot, sending me sprawling. This was repeated several times until I was allowed to call the others in to straighten up. Then it was time to go.

One night after dark, after the DI had obviously been drinking, we were called out of the Quonset huts in our underwear and forced to duck walk in a circle while the DI stood in the center, throwing the platoon guidon like a spear at anyone who faltered. He explained at the time that he was tired of hearing of captured Marines in Vietnam making anti-war statements and he was going to see to it that no matter how severely we might be tortured if we were captured, we would always know it had been worse in Boot Camp, and we would have survived—some of us.

Though many of our platoon were sent back for medical attention and picked up by other platoons, there was only one who died and that was not from mistreatment. He died of an infectious disease, spinal meningitis. Our platoon was put on quarantine for two weeks and instructed to refrain from physical exercise. Because we were not allowed to attend other scheduled events during that time we were restricted to our Quonset huts. The DIs, concerned that we might soften just before the final company competitions, used the time that we were in the huts to exercise us, not in the least concerned that constant fatigue might result in the onset of spinal meningitis.

Early on a few of the recruits decided that the treatment was inhumane and wrote letters to their congressmen. In the first week, apparently on a whim, a DI told the three of us from St. Paul that several tornadoes had destroyed the city killing hundreds of people. It was two weeks before we could find out it was a lie and our families and friends were safe. I chose, however, not to join the letter writers, knowing that my grasp on sanity was all too tenuous to cause further strain. Once the names of the letter writers filtered back through the chain of command the beatings were relentless for two full days before those men were sent to correctional platoon.

There were only about thirty of the original eighty left at the end of the twelve weeks. One of those graduated in a wheel chair after having his spleen broken in the last few days of Boot Camp.

Some would say that this no longer happens but I cannot believe it. No one can believe that it happened then; no one wants to believe humans could treat others in such a way. I would like to know it doesn't happen.

I am disturbed by the knowledge that what happened to me must surely be happening to others each day, as I am by the fact that it happened to me.

I learned long ago that I am not going to change the Marine Corps but as a high school teacher I have found that by sharing some of these things with my students I can certainly limit the destructive influence of the Corps. Perhaps in time, I can recover those fifty lost lives of platoon 3148 and make up for some of the loss suffered by the remaining thirty. My thoughts are often with those men though we were never allowed to speak to one another

> and I never learned their names. My thoughts are with the nameless ones who must be trying desperately to survive this day. Perhaps you know their names.

I am sure that some will think that this particular Marine was a troublemaker and probably did not do well in the Corps. We checked his record and learned that he did very well in all areas and even finished first in every school he attended.

The commandant, General Barrow, after reading this letter, wrote a note to the assistant commandant and to the deputy chief of staff for training as follows:

> I believe absolutely every word he says!! Indeed others during that period suffered worse experiences! Not only was the conduct wrong—*in every sense of the word*—but look at the mark it left on this individual and in turn the negative image he has portrayed to his students through the years!
>
> I want a really thoughtful letter for my signature. Beyond that I want his letter passed to both MCRD Commanding Generals with my request that they each give a thoughtful response (will also remind them that *it was that way*)!

The previous examples or theories of why we have had difficulties with abuse occurred to me after spending much time thinking about the subject. The final reason did not occur to me until after I had been with the Regiment for a while and had the opportunity to study some research conducted at San Diego on DIs.

The amount of real and perceived stress associated with being a DI is unbelievable. I had noticed that some DIs suffered from what must be called *burnout*, and it happened at specific times. They became frustrated, anxious, impatient, and short-tempered. That caused them to do things, which they would not otherwise consider, and it happened to some of the very best of DIs. For lack of a better word, I called it *spontaneous* abuse resulting from stress. Later chapters will cover this in greater detail and describe what we did to reduce it.

All the preceding descriptions contribute to explaining why the Corps has had and, at times, continues to have, difficulties in recruit training. Recruit abuse is not a significant problem at the present time, but the seeds for it to become one are present if the command does not insist on and constantly stress that the recruits must be trained with fairness, firmness, and dignity. The disparity in power between the DIs and recruits is much like that between children and parents. Just as children are almost totally dependent on their parents, so too are the recruits dependent on the DIs. The DIs are so motivated and dedicated to doing a good job that they can lose sight of reality and do things that they perceive as good for the Corps, even though it may be less than correct. Changing attitudes and reducing unnecessary stress are the only *long*-term solutions. All other remedies will result in short-term solutions, which will ultimately result in failure.

Changing those attitudes and reducing that *unnecessary* stress were seen as the major goals in attempting to develop the best Marines possible, and no opportunity to reinforce those goals was ever missed.

CHAPTER 3

The Drill Instructor

The storied DI is the key ingredient in the making of new Marines. He, more than anyone else, will make a lasting impression. Folklore suggests that he is a huge man with countless years of experience who has spent numerous years in the infantry. If only that were true! The average DI is 26.7 years old with 6.1 years of service. He comes from almost every military occupational specialty (MOS), with the infantry representing only 18 percent of the force. Administration, motor transport, supply, communication, military police, and aviation each represent about 7 percent, while the remainder comes from other fields. Approximately 10 percent have earned at least an associate degree, and 36 percent are of a minority group. Almost 80 percent are married. They are in excellent physical condition, and upon completion of DI school, they are experts on drill and numerous other subjects.

Although statistics are not available, I suspect that they are slightly larger than the average recruit. They are serious to a fault and totally dedicated to their task of training recruits. The average day for a DI commences at reveille, which for him is at least thirty minutes before the recruits. I'm sure that the recruits believe that he never sleeps.

He leads all the PT, conducts all instruction on the rifle, reinforces all other instruction, and is always present with the recruits. He is the first person that the recruits see in the morning and the last one at night.

He is very protective of "his platoon" and will spend untold hours attempting to develop the teamwork necessary for it to perform to standards as defined by the organization and by him. The senior DI is the father image and motivator while the assistant DIs are expected to be more aloof. That particular system has evolved over the years, and we have worked diligently to change it so that all the DIs could be motivators.

Certain Military Occupation Specialty (MOS) seemed to have more difficulty on the field than others. Generally speaking, the infantryman did not have the difficulty encountered by the other fields; however, when he did have trouble, it was normally other than minor infractions. It was rare for a supply man to be in trouble, and I never could determine why. The technical fields such as aviation and computers had more difficulty than the average, and I suspected that it resulted from the fact that they did not have the same opportunity to develop their leadership skills at the small-unit level, as did the infantryman.

The bachelors represented about half of those who ended up being relieved, although they were only 20 percent of the population. I believe that resulted from the fact that they did not have the opportunity to vent their frustrations with an understanding wife or that there was little outside pressure to be anywhere except with the platoon. They literally burned themselves out with work. That also received a great amount of attention in an attempt to correct this false sense of dedication by convincing the bachelor DIs that the Corps did not want or expect them to wear themselves out and, as a result, use bad judgment. It was not necessary for them to be with the platoon merely because they had no other place to be.

Unlike the other services, the Marines spend a great amount of time searching for the proper man to be a DI. Screening teams from each of the recruit depots are sent to all major commands throughout the Corps on a routine basis in search of possible candidates. Headquarters in Washington also screens records and submits names to the depots as possible candidates. Orders dictate that his commanding officer must personally interview each man selected for attendance at the DI school, and those units that do not comply receive a letter from the commandant. It normally does not happen a second time. The candidates must have at least one year left to serve on their current enlistment or be willing to extend, be in good physical condition, and have a good record.

Upon arrival at DI school, he is inspected, interviewed by a psychologist, and administered the MMPI, a very effective personality test. Almost without exception, a Marine is returned to his command if the psychologist suspects that he is at risk because of personality traits. The commanding officer (CO) is the final determining agent.

Shortly after each class was formed, I spoke to it, wished the Marines success, and outlined exactly what to expect. Prior to graduation, I spoke to them again with the emphasis on the quality of the recruits that they would be training. During their training phase, which lasted almost as long as Boot Camp, I visited each class at least every third day. I wanted them to be accustomed to seeing me on a routine basis.

The DI school is a very physical program; however, it is not a PT Academy. Upon initially assuming command, I noticed that the students conducted much of their PT in boots, and when asked why, the answer was that it contributed to the conditioning. That may have been true, but it also contributed to shin splints and stress fractures, which resulted in high attrition. The United States spends countless dollars in an attempt to develop the best running shoes in the world to reduce the shock of running on feet and joints. The boot was not designed for running and probably does a poor job of absorbing the shock associated with it. Because of that, I directed the school to eliminate running with boots.

Twice during their training, the DI students observed the recruits and worked with regular DIs for a day. That gave them the opportunity to actually work with the recruits and see for themselves what it really was like to be a DI. That also gave the battalions an opportunity to evaluate the new students. While in the school, the students trained together with a Gunnery Sergeant (Gy Sgt), who had been on the field for at least a year, as their squad leader and evaluator. They became experts on drill, CPR, the rifle, and all other subjects that the recruits learned. Practical application and written tests were administered throughout the course. Normally about 35 percent of the students failed to graduate. Even some of those who did graduate would not become effective DIs. In those cases, they were voided of their DI MOS (8511) and transferred—without harm to their careers. That had not always been the case.

That particular phenomenon came to my attention by accident. A DI was about to be relieved for cause, and upon questioning his commanding officer, it was learned that everyone knew that he could not be a DI. I asked why we had not submitted a package to have him relieved for Good of the Service (GOS). He responded that headquarters would not approve it if the DI had not done something wrong. I could not believe what I heard. "Do you mean to tell me that headquarters will not approve a GOS if we document it? I do not believe that they would rather have a DI possibly get all of us in trouble."

I spoke to the CG and informed him that I intended to submit a package to headquarters on a DI for a GOS. I then called headquarters and explained the reasoning and why I thought that it was important to have the GOS as a viable option. The package came back approved, as did all but two, which we submitted for the remainder of my tour. No longer would we carry a DI and wait for him to do something wrong and then relieve him for cause. In some cases, a DI would have a financial problem, which could not be solved while he remained on the field or perhaps he had a family problem, which could only be corrected by his spending more time with his family. It made little sense to retain him until the pressure caused him to do something stupid.

There are many tangible rewards for being a successful DI. Promotion boards look favorably upon a Marine who has had a successful tour on the drill field. The more successful DIs can be meritoriously promoted on the field. Additional clothing is issued to the DIs so that they always look sharp. Free cleaning also is provided, and they have their choice of duty stations upon transfer provided that there is a vacancy.

In talking to the DIs, it was brought to my attention that the DI option for duty station did not happen as it should. To them, it was a joke. Upon further investigation, it turned out to be a fact. Once again the CG was informed and he made a visit to headquarters. The following day, an action officer from headquarters arrived to determine the problem. From that time on, we had very little difficulty with the DI option; however, it still required close monitoring to insure that the system didn't break again. I recall on more than one occasion when I would ask a DI who was about to be transferred if he had received his option. Many times he would reply no, but that it did not matter. I would reply, "It may not matter to you, but it does to me. Where do you want to go?" In that manner, they learned that the command would ensure that promises were kept. Nothing is more important than fulfilling promises. That builds trust, and in this environment, trust is absolutely essential.

All in all, the DIs are truly among the finest enlisted men in the Corps and desire to train the best way possible. They are not inhuman and do not want to harm the recruits, but they do have a strong feeling about what makes a good Marine. They are intensely loyal to their fellow DIs and find it difficult to believe that some of them would harm a recruit. The pressures placed upon them are unbelievable although many of them are self-inflicted and inaccurate perceptions. Many of them feel that they must win at everything in order to be considered a good DI. They believe that they must spend every waking hour with the recruits even if it is nonproductive. Unfortunately, many believe that the officers are there to spy on them rather than help. Time is always critical, and they attempt to constantly maximize it. To praise good performance by recruits can be a sign of weakness and should only be used on rare occasions. We spent many hours attempting to correct those false perceptions. They often forgot what caused them to join the Corps and too frequently thought that these new recruits enlisted only for a job. I recall visiting a series at the dispensary, when it was receiving shots, and spending time talking to the DIs. The series looked sharp and moved quickly under the watchful eyes of the DIs. I asked one of the DIs why he thought they enlisted and he responded, "They are only here because they couldn't find a job, sir." I reached out and took a recruit by the arm and asked him when he had enlisted. At that particular time it was July, and the recruit responded that he had signed up in December.

I then asked another and he responded November, another January, December, and finally one said June. The DI seemed a little surprised, and I asked, "If they needed a job, what have they been doing for all the time since they enlisted? Very few arrive here the same month in which they enlist. Some of them wait for an entire year. Even if they were enlisting for a job, they could have gone into any of the services, but for whatever reason, they selected the Corps, and now it is up to us to turn them on." The other DIs listened as we had this conversation and appeared to understand its significance. At any rate, I never lost the opportunity to talk to the DIs about the recruits and their motivations and background. It was vital that the DIs had a positive feeling about the recruits if we were to make any impact on the attitudes.

Throughout my entire tour, I never had a DI relieved that I had spoken to about recruit training one-on-one. That merely reinforced my belief that they wanted to perform well, and if shown the proper way, they would do it.

They were so motivated and so dedicated that at times they could not understand why everyone did not feel the same way. They forgot that the recruits just did not know all that we wanted them to know. It was up to the command to constantly stress that it was our job to train them and make Marines out of them.

During one of our many fireside chats, the topic came up about the recruits not being able to perform satisfactorily. The DIs felt that they just did not care. They were absolutely serious and could not understand why it took so long for some of the recruits to learn some of the movements and information that we demanded. I tried to put it in terms that would be easy to understand.

"You all know how to write, and you all know what each letter looks like. Let me ask you to try something when you return to your barracks. Sit down and write the alphabet with the opposite hand that you normally use. I can assure you that it will take longer and that it will not look as good. It will not be because you do not want to write well or that you are not motivated, but rather that you just did not have the practice using your other hand. The recruits are the same. They need time to practice in order to perfect what we are attempting to teach them. They want to do it, they just can't. Let me give you another example. Most of you have played baseball when you were in school. You know how to hold the bat and you know how to hit the ball when it is pitched. Now let's take you to a major league team and let you try to hit the ball as pitched from a professional. The chances are that you will not be successful because he throws the ball too fast or it does peculiar things as it moves toward the plate. It's not that you are not motivated or that you don't know how to do it, but rather, you need more practice if you are ever to become proficient. Couldn't the recruits be in the same boat? It takes time!"

Not all these talks were successful, but I am sure that they caused many of the men to rethink some of their attitudes. Since they are among the best in the Corps, it must have had a little effect.

CHAPTER 4

Initial Changes

One of the areas in which the DIs take exceptional pride is drill. They are the experts, and the competition among the platoons is keen. There are two drill competitions: The first is held immediately prior to going to the rifle range with the newest DI drilling the platoon. The final drill is held during the last week before graduation and the senior DI drills the platoon.

I had noticed that at drill, the platoons rarely marched at the flank, and they normally marched at port arms. That caused several problems. The arm swings were much more difficult to perfect because both hands were on the rifle at port arms. It also caused the recruits to lean back to such a degree that it was unnatural. Since they didn't spend much time at right or left shoulder arms, the rifle carriage also suffered.

The fastest way to change anything, especially in Boot Camp, was to make it important. At graduation, the series passed in review in column, which was rather simple to do. I decided to change the procedure so that the platoons passed in review on line. When on line, the platoon must march with about ten or twelve men beside the side of each other rather than the four while in column. In addition, it's much easier to see and correct the arm swing and posture. I knew that if it was necessary to pass in review on line, at graduation, then the platoons would spend more time during drill practice, and as a result, the drill would improve. I spoke to the battalion commanders and told them what I intended to do and why. They were not that pleased. I also spoke to the general and outlined my plan so that he would not be surprised.

It was expected that the first few graduations would be ragged as the DIs and platoons adjusted, but that was the short-term loss for the long-term gain. I also spent time talking to the DIs and explaining that I intended to change the pass in review and why. It did not meet with much enthusiasm.

One of the many techniques that I have used over the years is to maintain a diary with cryptic notes to refresh my memory at a later time.

It became rather useful when I attempted to recount particular events at a later date.

Diary, July 16, 1982

The pass in review at the flank for graduation went fine. It will work and drill will improve.

We started before the end of July with the new ceremony—the DIs were up in arms and insisted that it would not work. Change is always difficult, but here it is even worse because they believe everything is traditional. Actually, the first ceremony looked pretty good. The lines were not perfect, but that was expected. On one occasion, the general's son, who was home from college for the summer, sat in the bleachers to watch one of the graduations. He reported to his father that he must return to the pass in review in column because the DIs did not like the other way. The general and I both had a good laugh about that.

During the next several months, I spoke to countless DIs and asked if they knew why we had changed the ceremony. The answers were rather humorous, but the one that came up the most was that *I just wanted it to be different.* I went into great detail explaining why it had been changed and its purpose. It took quite a while, but it finally took effect and the drill did improve.

At one time, one of the DIs told me that I should not be surprised if the general received a call from the commandant and was told to go back to the old way.

I told him that I was sure that the commandant had more important things to worry about than how we passed in review, but that if a call ever did come, we would comply. The call never came.

Diary, October 5, 1982

The CG called and said to go ahead with putting the hats back on Support Battalion DIs.

As the DIs became more comfortable with me, they started to open up. One of the first things that they brought to my attention was the wearing of the DI hats. The DIs assigned to Support Battalion were not authorized to wear them. To the uninitiated, that may not seem like a big issue, but it was. When a DI graduated from DI School, he was issued a campaign hat, which he wore at all times unless he was under some type of investigation or had been relieved. No one else was authorized to wear them, and a lot of pride went with the privilege.

If a DI was reassigned to Support Battalion, he was not authorized to wear his hat. It seemed that that particular ruling had been in effect for quite some time, and to me it made little sense. In fact, there had been some individuals in the past that thought that if all the hats were placed on the parade deck and burned, then all problems with the DIs would disappear. The same type of thinking probably resulted in the not wearing of campaign hats in Support Battalion.

Support Battalion had administrative control over all those personnel who were not directly assigned to a training battalion. That included the Field Training Unit (FTU); the Instructional Training Unit (ITU); Casual, where the recruits went for discharge processing; Receiving, where the recruits were housed upon arrival; and the Special Training Division (STD). Drill instructors would normally be assigned to Support Battalion for about six months and then return to a training battalion.

The Regiment could not function without Support Battalion, and yet their DIs felt like second-rate citizens. Their argument was that they had successfully completed DI school and had done nothing wrong and yet they could not wear the hat that distinguished them as DIs. Their complaint made sense to me.

I spoke with General McMonagle and outlined the problem and then recommended that we give the hats back to the DIs in Support Battalion except for Casual and Receiving. If it went as I expected in Support Battalion, then we would authorize Casual and Receiving to wear campaign hats also. He agreed, and the word was passed—the morale went up immediately.

Now that the problem of hats was settled, I could look at another problem associated with Support Battalion, which was the quality of DIs being assigned. The general consensus was that if one were transferred to Support Battalion, you were not considered to be a good DI. Unfortunately in too many cases that had been true. There were 126 DIs assigned to Support Battalion, and the order outlining the assignment stated that it would be for six to nine months. In too many cases, a DI was assigned and remained until his tour was complete. In fact, some of these DIs even extended for a six—or twelve-month period and remained in Support Battalion. I called the battalion commanders to my office and explained that we needed good DIs in Support Battalion. It should be used as a reward or an opportunity to give a DI who was getting tired a break from the recruits for a few months. They all agreed and added that they already sent good DIs to Support Battalion. I said, "Fine, there are 126 DIs in Support Battalion and you can have any one of them back, the only requirement is that I need a replacement."

Out of the 126 DIs, I received the name of only one man that they wanted back. My suspicions were confirmed, and I immediately outlined procedures to correct the problem.

The order was rewritten so that it specifically outlined the rules for assignment to Support Battalion and that there would be no exceptions. Then we instituted a procedure to assign a few new DIs from each graduating DI class directly to Support Battalion for their initial six months. I intended to change the perception that Support Battalion was a bad assignment.

The only restrictions were that a new DI could not be assigned to Casual or Receiving. Those two areas were time bombs which could go off at any time, and the DIs assigned to them must be of known quality. In addition, any DI who desired to extend needed the approval of the CO of Support Battalion as well as the battalion he came from because that is where he would spend his extension. It took a while before the total benefits could be seen, but it was well worth the effort. Ultimately, Support Battalion DIs received as many meritorious promotions as any other battalion did by the time the changes reached fruition.

During my constant travels throughout the Regiment, I spoke and listened to countless DIs and officers. As I did this, I can't say how many DIs that I discovered violating the regulations, not seriously, but violations nonetheless. On each occasion, we would talk at great length on how important it was to train the recruits properly. On one occasion, I stopped by the recruit Post Exchange (PX) and walked around the side of the building. One of the assistant DIs had about half of his platoon conducting incentive physical training (IPT). IPT was a series of exercises that the DIs could require the recruits to perform if they were not responding up to the standards of the DIs. The exercises and conditions for them were closely controlled. Regulations stated that only the senior DI could IPT more than ten recruits at once. The DI turned, saw me, and almost had a stroke! He immediately called the platoon to attention and reported. I asked what he was doing and why. He stammered a little, and then we talked, or I should say that I talked and he listened. The conversation went for quite a while, and finally I asked if he understood why it was so important to do what was right. I might add that this particular DI left the field about one year later as a staff sergeant instead of only as a sergeant.

He was one of the first DIs that I found not doing exactly what was right, and in all cases except one, we talked. Not a single DI that I spoke to under those circumstances ever left the drill field except for his normal rotation.

In the movie *The DI* Jack Webb portrayed a tough drill instructor who, at one point, had a recruit search for a sand flea that he had slapped from his face. It was quite a humorous scene for those who had ever experienced the discomfort of those terrible creatures. These fleas are absolutely unbelievable, and they thrive on human flesh. They are attracted by carbon dioxide, so they flock to the recruits whenever they are outdoors. Their bite leaves a red welt, which lasts, and it itches.

During PT, they become the scourges for both recruits and DIs alike. I recall in my own Boot Camp that it was a crime to swat a flea. Allowing these insects to eat their fill was somehow expected to instill discipline. I can accept that up to a point, because an individual should not be moving around while at the position of attention or in an ambush site.

My DI would march us into a field and require us to remain at attention for extended periods of time just to allow the fleas to eat their fill. There comes a time, though, when the mind can think only of relief from the agony. Before that occurs, the better DIs allow the recruits to "wipe them off" and then return to the tasks at hand.

Diary, January 20, 1983

Talked, rather listened, to 1stSgt Moore and left there on cloud nine. If all DIs thought that way, we would have no problems.

First Sergeant Moore was a superb leader. He had been a cook prior to becoming a first sergeant, and he knew how to lead and spent an extraordinary amount of time sharing his techniques with his subordinates. He was a slightly built black Marine who enjoyed talking about Marines and how to make new ones. We had many discussions about leadership and how to make a Marine.

On one of my many visits to *his* office, the topic turned to the sand flea and its effects upon the recruits. "Colonel," he said, "I watched two platoons outside waiting to be inspected. Each of the platoons had a DI with a varying amount of experience on the field. The day was hot and muggy, and the sand fleas were out in force. One of the platoons stood at rigid attention while the DI had them respond to his questions. After a while, one of the recruits in the rear would relieve himself by swiping at a sand flea on his face or arm. As he watched, more and more of the recruits resorted to the same technique. All the while, the DI berated them about their lack of discipline. The other platoon stood at parade rest as the DI also asked it questions. No one moved, because periodically the DI called it to attention, gave it rest and told the recruits to 'wipe them off.'

"After watching this for a while, I called the DI who had the platoon standing at rigid attention into my office. 'Watch those two platoons and tell me what you see,' I told him. He looked a little bewildered but complied. I then asked him which platoon was learning more and taking advantage of the time available and which platoon appreciated the leadership more. This DI could see exactly what I attempted to show him without losing face."

First Sergeant Moore went on to say that it is not being easy on the recruits but, rather, smart to allow them to concentrate on the questions rather than the sand fleas. Those recruits who stood at rigid attention until they no longer could stand it were learning bad habits that could have been avoided. Now that's what I call a leader. First Sergeant Moore was not easy, but he was fair and realistic.

His company had fewer problems than any company in the Regiment, and I believe it was because of the way he used small incidents like this, which occurred constantly. For the most part, it also was a happy company. First Sergeant Moore could be seen throughout his area checking on training, and he was sure to make corrections whenever needed. His standards were high, and everyone knew what they were.

The only staff NCO who had a better appreciation of leadership than First Sergeant Moore was my sergeant major (Sgt Maj), McCormick. He stood well over six feet and weighed in at about 230 pounds and looked every part the Marine. Naturally he had been on the drill field before and shared many of his experiences with me. He did not mince words, and everyone knew exactly where he stood. To say that he was my senior enlisted advisor was a gross understatement. He was studying for his degree in counseling and was truly a student in human behavior.

We got along famously because we thought a lot alike and he had the knack for putting people at ease.

I recall one time when we were discussing the DIs and he gave me his opinion of the "hard A." The *hard A* was the term used for the experienced assistant drill instructor in each of the platoons. He said, "The DIs are constantly searching for methods to be recognized as effective DIs. Years ago, there were probably two DIs each inspecting a squad, and one of them was a little more detailed than the other and found many more discrepancies. He was praised by his seniors for his diligence, and so the next inspection, he repeated the routine. After a while, it became more and more difficult each time to find discrepancies, and so he created them in order to receive the praise. The recruits were required to remove Irish pennants from inside their clothing (Irish pennants are loose pieces of thread), shine the back of their brass, and other outlandish time-consuming tasks.

Under no circumstances would he ever praise the recruits for a job well done because according to him, that would spoil the recruits. Since this DI seemed to be successful, his methods were copied by newer DIs and so it went. It made sense to me because I could see some of those actions taking place. The sergeant major was truly a student of behavior and always looked for reasons behind various actions.

Prior to each series graduation, the series officers and senior DIs came to my office to summarize the series performance and to cover any areas that could possibly help following series. We kept statistics on every aspect of the training. The summary showed how many recruits started, how many would graduate, the average score on the Physical Fitness Test, the number of swimmers, average age, average IQ, level of education, rifle qualification percentage, and any other indicator which could assist in predicting success or improving training. Some of these discussions lasted several hours as we tried to share techniques and allow the DIs to ventilate. Sergeant Major McCormick would get together with the DIs after this and, on many occasions, cover some of the material from the perspective of a former DI and a present sergeant major. He was absolutely magnificent. I'm sure that he shared stories about what he and I talked about as we toured the Regiment.

CHAPTER 5

The Studies

Diary, September 30, 1982

The studies from Dr. Sarasen in Calif. arrived today. There are some interesting data in them.

I had heard about some ongoing studies conducted on recruit training that had been initiated at Recruit Depot San Diego following the congressional hearings in 1976, and so I asked if they could be sent to me for reading. The data from these studies had been accumulating for years, but no one had seemed to be interested since they were conducted by two psychologists from Washington State. These studies started by analyzing the stress on the recruits, and after a period of time, they realized that the problem was not the recruits but, rather, the DIs.

Several of the studies were sent, and after reading them, it was obvious that they coincided with what happened at Parris Island. Two periods were critical for the DIs—the three-month period and the one-year period. The studies did not offer much rationale for why the DIs changed psychologically and physiologically—but change they did. The DIs' blood pressure and pulse rates both increased along with a feeling of time consciousness and being less tolerant and more critical.

Since all my graduate study had been in counseling and behavior and I had read much on those topics along with working in the environment, I thought that I knew why these two periods were critical for the DIs. At the three-month period, the new DI had just completed his first platoon, and if he had done well, the pressure was on to continue to do well. If he had not done well, then even more pressure was on to improve or possibly suffer the consequences of not being accepted. At the one-year mark, he could be becoming tired and perhaps frustrated. At the one-year mark, it also was the first really valid opportunity to be considered for meritorious promotion since these promotions were dependent almost entirely on performance as a DI. By that time, he probably had been working many extra hours for weeks on end without a break. The number of DIs at Parris Island who got into trouble at the one-year period was high. *It all made sense!* What we needed to do was back off a little and try to do something to prevent it from happening rather than waiting until a DI was in trouble.

The studies covered a wide range of areas including the attrition of recruits during training. They looked at high attrition and low attrition DIs (those DIs who historically lost many recruits and those who lost fewer for whatever reason) and compared the results of the platoons to determine if there was a difference in performance. One would suspect that if the DIs with high attrition had eliminated those recruits who could pull platoon performance down, then those platoons would do better statistically. The results did not support that thesis. There was no significant statistical difference among the platoons.

Rather than stop there, it was decided to take a look at how these new Marines from different platoons did after they left Boot Camp and joined their first units. It was discovered that those individuals who graduated from high-attrition platoons continued to attrit at a high level, 41 percent. Those individuals who graduated from the low-attrition platoons suffered 22 percent attrition. No cause was offered for this phenomenon, but again I believed that I could offer a logical reason. Those individuals who came from the low-attrition platoons were trained and given a sense of belonging so that when things became tough, they hung in there. The other individuals were not provided that sense of belonging and when it became tough for them and they needed to make choices without the ever-present DI, they couldn't handle it.

Now I could show the DIs some statistics and argue more for training the recruits rather than attriting them. There were some DIs who always had high attrition, and they felt that their Marines were better. During my following discussions with the DIs, I stressed the meaning of the statistics. It went something like this, "Would you accept the fact that chance being what it is, that there are times when a DI would receive more than his fair share of highly motivated, coordinated, dedicated, disciplined, and physically fit recruits? When that happened, one would expect that the attrition would be low. There are also times, with chance being what it is, that the DI would receive more than his fair share of recruits who lack those characteristics and when that happened, one would expect high attrition. Normally one could expect to receive his fair share of all types of recruits, and attrition should be normal."

They all nodded in agreement at the rationale. I then went on to say," If you give me the names of the DIs and series officers, I will tell you what the attrition will be before the first recruit enters the gate, and I will not miss it by more than five recruits. I can and have done that because there are some teams who would attrit six out of the twelve disciples if they came through the gate. That is not right, it is not fair, and it is not what the Corps desires. There are some DIs who believe that they can tell if a recruit will make it merely by looking at him. If that were true, we should make him a recruiter and save the Corps a lot of time and money."

The DIs looked at me in amazement, but then they knew that I normally did not jest with something this important. They thought of, and I'm sure that they could name some of the DIs who fit the bill. I also did this at final drill when the senior DI marched his platoon in a competition with the other three platoons in the series, and I was correct almost all the time because I had observed them drilling and conducting all other trainings.

In a later chapter, I will describe what we did about the stress problem and how effective that it was. The results were far beyond what we had hoped them to be.

CHAPTER 6

The Schedule

Boot Camp is the most significant experience that a young man undergoes in his entire career in the Corps. Members of the other services complete their basic training and much is soon forgotten; Boot Camp lives with a Marine forever. I doubt if anyone who has completed Boot Camp cannot vividly recall his drill instructor and the experiences he underwent during that intensive time. Many successful men in all walks of life attribute their success in life to Boot Camp and the Marines. It has always been so and will continue.

Even though the quality of the recruits continues to rise, attrition in Boot Camp remains at about 13 percent. That is because there are fully qualified individuals who are not willing to undergo the sacrifices necessary to become a United States Marine, and since the training is intensive, there are injuries. Most of those depart during the first two weeks before they really give themselves the opportunity to see what the Corps is truly about. For those who remain, there is a challenging and rewarding experience ahead.

The training program that turns them into Marines is fifty-six training days long, not counting a week of mess and maintenance where they either work in the mess hall or go on working parties throughout the base cutting grass and cleaning the base in order to save money on labor. The average recruit spends eleven weeks at the recruit depot before he becomes a full-fledged Marine.

Graduating Marines achieve the following results in Boot Camp:

Rifle Qualification—99.4%
Second-Class Swimmer—22.0%
Third-Class Swimmer—66.0%
Essential Subjects—100%
Physical Fitness Test—245+ points (300 is max)

In addition, they all run five miles, undergo extensive nuclear, biological, and chemical (NBC) training, negotiate obstacle and confidence courses, and spend seven days in the field undergoing individual combat training.

As always, arriving recruits are apprehensive, not knowing exactly what to expect. They have heard and read about Boot Camp and anticipate the worst. After the eleven weeks, they leave highly motivated and looking forward to their first assignment. They, like the thousands who have preceded them, are Marines, and they are proud.

All their accomplishments are achieved through much hard work. Nothing is given; all must be earned. The program is exceptionally detailed and long. Although the training schedule covers only ten hours per day, the full schedule covers sixteen hours.

The recruits generally arrive at Parris Island at night between 2300 and 0100. They assemble by train and plane in Charleston, South Carolina, and are bused onto Parris Island. Upon arrival, they are processed for about three days before they are turned over to their DIs for the beginning of training.

When they are turned over to their DIs, there are about three days of what is referred to as "forming." The formal schedule has yet to start. They are issued rifles, receive more inoculations, and are introduced to the basic daily routine.

EVENT	**MON-SAT**	**SUN/HOL**
Reveille	0500	0600
Personal Hygiene/Police		
Morning Meal	0500-0650	0600-0700
Sick Call	0600	
Training Commences	0700	—
Church Call	—*	
Noon Meal	1130	1130
Sick Call	1300 (Bn. Area)	1130
Training Commences	1300	—
Evening Meal	1700	1700
Commanders' Time	1730-1930	1730-1930
DI Hygiene Inspection	1930-1950	1930-1950
Recruit Free Time	1950-2050	1950-2050
Final Muster/Devotions	2050-2100	2050-2100

*As prescribed in current bulletins for religious activities published by the chaplain.

The actual training program is divided into three phases. Phase I is concerned with teaching fundamental drills, military subjects, physical training, swimming, leadership, and the rifle.

During Phase I, the recruits are administered the initial strength test to determine if they are in adequate condition to continue training with their platoon. When I initially arrived, it consisted of running one mile in less than ten minutes, completing thirty-five sit-ups in less than two minutes, and completing at least one pull-up. Those might not sound like difficult tasks, but about 10 percent could not do them. The recruits unable to pass were transferred to the Physical Conditioning Platoon (PCP) where the emphasis was on a conditioning program, which normally took about three weeks to successfully complete. Phase I normally lasted for three or four weeks depending on the number of recruits at the command.

In Phase II, the recruits spent two weeks at the rifle range learning how to fire their weapons followed by one week of mess and maintenance. The first week on the range consisted of snapping-in practice where they learned the different shooting positions, how to aim and shoot the rifle, and safety regulations. The second week was spent shooting the rifle. Those recruits who did not qualify on record day, which was the fifth day of firing, were transferred to the Marksmanship Training Platoon (MTP) where they spent one additional week of shooting. A series normally qualified 85-92 percent of its recruits on record day and up to 100 percent by the end of the following week. Those recruits who did qualify spent the following week on mess duty or working parties around the base and then proceeded to the final phase.

Phase III is packed full of requirements, including the final physical fitness test, five-mile run, inspections, individual combat training, academic testing, morning colors ceremony, final drill evaluation, and graduation. Each of these events occurs after much training and practice with each day full of difficult and challenging tasks. The members of the platoon work closer together as a team, and all activities are conducted with an eye toward developing the two most important elements in Boot Camp: pride and discipline.

The recruit training task would be much easier if pride and discipline could be taught, but they cannot. They must be developed and instilled. Those are the qualities that make a Marine and why Boot Camp is so important. If the recruit depots are successful in instilling them, then the Marine probably will be successful for the remainder of his enlistment.

Although the schedule is quite full, there remains room for flexibility for those DIs who know how to use their imagination. It is amazing how inventive they can be. We have the capability for both reward and punishment in Boot Camp, but we are much more reluctant in handing out the rewards. I started asking about how we rewarded the recruits for superior performance and was met with many blank stares. One DI replied, "You can't do that, sir, because they take advantage of everything that they are given." I paused for a second and then asked, "What do we give them?" He looked puzzled and thought, but said nothing. That's exactly what we give them, nothing. On another occasion I asked a DI, and he replied, "Sir, you can't do that. My last platoon won initial drill, and it took me three days to tighten it up." I smiled to myself, for what he was saying in effect was that his platoon had won the most important event during Phase I and he had punished it. He went on to say that for the final drill it had come in last. Again I smiled to myself for I would have been surprised if there had been any other result.

For the next several weeks, I continued to talk to the DIs about rewards and the possibility of extra free time for superior performance. "The recruits know when they have had a good day. Wouldn't it be effective if the DI called them together and told them how proud he was of them, and then gave them an extra thirty minutes free time? I suspected that the recruits would probably talk about it and wonder if the same would happen if they did well the following day. If that happened, do it again. Now human nature being what it is, I'm sure that after a few days the recruits would believe that they would receive the extra free time each night. When they did not a have a good day, don't give them the extra time. Again I'm sure that there would be some talk about not receiving additional free time. One would probably say that they did not deserve it, but perhaps they could get it back if they had another good day tomorrow."

I could have ordered this to be done, but that was not the purpose. If it were ordered, it would not work. In order to have effective procedures, the men must embrace the routine as their own. I was content to be patient and wait for one DI to try it and discover what happened. There was no doubt in my mind that when he saw the results, he would pass the word and then others would do it also. Why did they not see that rewards produce better results than punishment? The gentle push continued as I tried to convince the DIs to use the incentive at their disposal. I told them that when an operating battalion goes to the field and does well, the battalion commander might grant special liberty as a reward. Naturally the battalion is elated, and chances are that the next time that it goes to the field, it will bust its tail to do well again. It is a tool that is available to you, and you are foolish if you do not use every tool available to produce the very best Marine possible.

Diary, August 3, 1982

> *Finally found a DI who used the extra thirty minutes free time. It worked!*

After a period of time, I met a DI at the rifle range who asked if I recalled talking to him about the rewards. He said that he had been doing it with his platoon and it had literally run off with all the competitions during Phase I. He beamed as he related how he went about motivating his recruits. As time passed, more of the DIs used various methods of rewards as incentive and were pleased with the results. Patience had paid off. Humans are typically the same everywhere, and they respond to both punishments and rewards the same.

CHAPTER 7

The Regiment

Touring the Regiment is a tedious and time-consuming task because elements of it utilize the entire island. The island consists of about eight thousand acres of land and over four thousand are available for training. The Regiment consists of three training battalions and a support battalion. Each training battalion consists of two companies and each company can have up to five series. A series consists of four platoons and a platoon has between sixty to ninety recruits. The series team consists of a series officer, an assistant series officer, a chief drill instructor, and three or four DIs for each platoon.

The size of the platoons fluctuates during the year with larger platoons in the summer and the smaller platoons in the winter. Normally, there are several thousand more recruits in training during the summer after high schools graduate, and thus the platoons are larger. There was a time during the Vietnam War when platoons had more than one hundred recruits. I cannot imagine trying to train a platoon that large, especially when one considers that during the war there were companies in combat with about the same number of men as a platoon in Boot Camp. One should be able to appreciate the problems associated with trying to develop that many men into Marines in such a short period of time. It is difficult for the DIs just to learn the names of the recruits with that many people. When the platoons are large, all the facilities are stretched to the limit. The classrooms can barely hold the large numbers and then only if the chairs are placed closer together.

Unlike the training battalions, Support Battalion does not have series. It controls the swimming pool; instructional training unit (ITU) for all formal teaching; field training unit (FTU) for all field training; and the special training division (STD). STD consists of the marksmanship training platoon (MTP), physical conditioning platoon (PCP), and the medical rehabilitation platoon (MRP).

PCP was located in a barracks at the rifle range. During my initial briefings, I had visited PCP and did not feel comfortable. Something bothered me and I could not put my finger on it; however, with the rush of trying to learn all that I could about the Regiment, there was no time to dwell on what it was. At a later date, I received another briefing and just to be sure that I had not made a mistake, I returned to PCP. I had the director explain the program again. Wow! Now I knew what had bothered me. When a recruit started physical training with a regular platoon, we did it gradually. For the first five days, he ran one and a half miles, for the next five days he ran two miles, for the following five days he ran two and a half miles, and finally, he ran three miles. That allowed the body time to adjust and be acclimatized. At PCP we made them run three miles the first day. We already knew that they could not run a mile and now we expected them to run three. The attrition at PCP was high and it was no wonder. I told the director that the program would change immediately. We would abide by the time schedule.

It amazed me that something so simple could have been missed. We were lucky that a recruit had not been hurt. Later there would be many other changes at PCP. Joe Gieck, the trainer at the University of Virginia, was a friend of mine since we had attended graduate school together. Naturally he was an expert on training and conditioning. I wrote him a letter and made him an offer that he could not refuse. I told him that if he came to PI, I would show him how we made Marines, and in return, I wanted him to take a look at our PT program, especially the one at PCP. It worked! Joe did come and we both received an education. He recommended a program that would better help us get a man into shape. We used high-intensity/low-intensity days for PT and could see the difference almost immediately.

In addition, we purchased more nautilus-type equipment for use at PCP. While that progressed, we continued to search for better means to maintain motivation while conditioning the recruits for their return to training.

Captain Trout, the officer in charge at PCP, noticed a trend in the assignment of recruits to PCP, which apparently led to failure. Immediately after the initial strength test, the recruits started their PT for the next five days with a run of one and one half miles. If they fell out three times, they were transferred to PCP. The greatest majority joined before training day seven. That seemed to indicate that although they could run the first mile, they were not in sufficient shape to start training. We conducted additional research and learned that one and one half miles was a better indicator of minimum conditioning. The initial strength test was changed and guidance given to the command that anyone who could not cover the distance in thirteen and one half minutes would be transferred to PCP. We felt that the motivation problem at PCP resulted from the recruits being with their regular platoons too long before transfer. Let me explain.

A recruit platoon is like a family. The relationships become extremely close and strong in a short period of time. When a recruit is dropped, it is like taking him from his mother's breast. If they were dropped on the first day, perhaps we would sever the link before it developed too strongly.

The series team also was instructed to give the recruits a pep talk prior to the transfer about this being a setback rather than a complete failure. At PCP, each newly arrived recruit was given a buddy, who was a highly motivated recruit designated to make the transition as smooth as possible.

Talking with PT experts, we learned that a schedule of twenty-one days would normally be the average amount of time required for improving the conditioning of men so that they could return to training. We started to train smarter rather than easier. Now we could tell the recruits about how long they could expect to remain in PCP. It ceased to be open-ended. In addition, the normal academics for Phase I were covered at PCP so that the recruits progressed in other areas in addition to physical conditioning and many of them returned to other than training day one when they left PCP.

The change in attrition and attitudes was unbelievable. As we continued to refine the training, we attempted more and more innovative schemes. We allowed the DIs to send those recruits who still needed conditioning but were in good enough shape to remain with their platoons to PCP for the week while the remainder of the platoon was on mess and maintenance and then return to their platoons.

Prior to the start of these innovations, the DIs were very skeptical about receiving PCP recruits because they historically had not done well. A former DI, retired Sergeant Major Skinner, operated the depot physical fitness center.

He also had much nautilus equipment for use in bodybuilding. I had gone there and asked him to put me through the paces in order to make my own determination. That left little doubt in my mind that it worked. When I found a DI who was skeptical, I directed him to see Skinner and let him put him through the paces and then tell me that it was easy. Soon, many of the DIs actively sought to have PCP graduates assigned to their platoons because they were motivated and they were in shape.

The three training battalions all were located at the main portion of the base; however, the Third Battalion was the farthest from the headquarters. It spent more time in movement to classrooms, clothing issue, shots, and other evolutions. The additional lost time could be made up by taking advantage of the movement time to drill, and at other times when battalions squeezed in additional drill, the Third Battalion could spend it reinforcing knowledge such as rifle nomenclature, first aid, history, traditions, etc. Third Battalion was also the only battalion that did not have air-conditioned barracks since they were the oldest buildings.

CHAPTER 8

Individual Combat Training and Rifle Range

In Phase II, when the recruits went to the rifle range, the first weapon that they fired was the .45-caliber pistol. That took place on the afternoon of the first day. That is probably our most dangerous weapon, and the recruits were not accustomed to range procedures. There seemed to be a lot of wasted time, and it detracted from teaching the rifle. Although the qualification percentages were high with the rifle, the recruits still did not seem to fully understand all aspects of the sight adjustment or other finer points in shooting. We needed more time! I decided to remove the pistol firing from Phase II and shift it to the field training in Phase III.

During my many visits to the range, I had never seen the use of the Belgian Sight or triangulation during snapping-in. The Belgian Sight is a device that fits on the rear sight of the rifle so that a coach is able to see exactly what the shooter sees. In that way, the coach can determine if the shooter understands sight picture and sight alignment. These techniques add to better understanding of shooting, and they were reinstituted along with a talk to the DIs. "I do not care what the qualification percentages are. We must teach the recruits how to shoot, and if we do that properly, the percentages will take care of themselves. I am aware that a CG in the past had required the DI of any platoon shooting below 90 percent to report to him and explain why. I also am aware that no DI ever had to report. That is not what I want. Percentages be dammed, if necessary, I'll take the heat. We must teach them to shoot, not just get a score." It had the desired effect.

In conjunction with changing the range schedule, we took a long look at the time and sequence of field training. Over the years, the various commanders had made numerous adjustments, and now the sequence did not follow logically. It was not the normal building block, and there was little flexibility. I likened it to a small home that was quite suitable for newlyweds until the children started to arrive. The father added rooms and baths, which made it acceptable. If he could have built the end product from the beginning, the design would have been much different. We would design the field training so that it made more sense and flowed logically.

As an example, on the last day in the field, the troops marched to the range and combat fired their rifles at pop-up targets using battle sights. They then returned to their barracks at about 1700, in time for evening meal, followed by a short period of time to clean their gear and rifles, which had been in the field for five days. Naturally, that was insufficient time, and the DIs were on the horns of a dilemma. Many of the DIs used the free time of the recruits to accomplish the impossible task. That was not fair, and when they were caught, they paid the price.

In the middle of the five days, the recruits went on a ten-mile hike and followed that with half a day of physically strenuous squad tactics. The new schedule took all these matters into consideration and adjusted accordingly.

Diary, October 15, 1982

The new ICT started yesterday. So far it is better than expected. WO. Jerrold, the range officer, can see the difference in motivation, rifle cleanliness, hits on target, alertness, etc, Hoorah!

The first day was spent at the pistol range and combat firing of rifles. The recruits had already been to the rifle range, so the range procedures posed no problems, and they knew how to shoot their rifles so the combat firing was simpler. Following that, they hiked to Page Field, set up their bivouac, and prepared for the following day. The schedule flowed logically, and on the final day of seven days, they had their ten-mile hike, which had been preceded during the week by shorter hikes to toughen the feet. The hike ended at the barracks by about 1000, leaving the remainder of the day to clean their weapons and gear. The DIs were no longer coerced into violating regulations, and the recruits learned more with fewer foot injuries from hiking. In addition, we had hospital corpsmen at the squad bay to check the recruits' feet so that there would be fewer problems later, and we discovered small blisters before they became large.

One of the very subtle aspects of the field training taught the recruits how to live in the field and to prepare the food to be as tasty as possible. It should not be eaten cold but, rather, heated in order to gain the maximum benefit from it. Some of the officers and DIs felt that it made the recruits harder if they were not allowed to heat the food. Their rationale escaped me, and much emphasis was placed on how to prepare the food.

As I visited a series on its first day in the field, I spoke to the series officer and asked if the recruits had heated their chow. He assured me that they had; however, when I started to speak to the recruits, it became obvious that they had not. They did not have the heat tabs to do the job. I spoke to the officer again and explained the importance of chow and doing what was correct. First, it tasted much better, second, it was more nutritious, and third, it developed the habit of heating the chow, which would be essential in extreme cold. There was no raised voice or chewing out but, rather, an instructional monologue on "taking care of the troops."

It just so happened that almost a week later I was in the mess hall when that particular series entered for lunch. It had hiked in from the field almost two hours earlier, and yet not one of the recruits had been given the opportunity to wash his hands or change clothes before going to the mess hall. I was livid and searched for the officers responsible. Fortunately for them, they were not present, or I would have relieved them on the spot.

I called the battalion and ordered those officers to be in my office immediately. The first to arrive was the battalion commander, who wanted to know what the problem was about. "I am tired of a few officers and DIs treating the recruits like animals. I will not tolerate it." He had never seen me angry before, and it came as a shock. The officers reported in a short period in the uniform of the day freshly showered and shaved. In comparison to the recruits whom they had sent to the mess, they were immaculate.

Normally, I put the men at ease when I want to talk, but in their case, I kept them at attention. There had been sufficient time elapse such that I had cooled off. I looked both of them in the eyes and then started, "I would not treat a dog the way that you treated your recruits. Apparently you do not understand that they are United States Marine Recruits. They are not pigs, or shitheads, or hogs, or any other demeaning name. They are recruits, and we are responsible for them. I will not tolerate their being treated with other than dignity. You would never dream of treating Marines like that, and by God, you will not do it to recruits. If you had been in the mess when I found your series, I would have relieved you on the spot. If I ever find either of you not doing what is correct, I will act accordingly. Do you understand?" They replied "Yes, sir" and were dismissed. They had seen a side of me that does not surface very often, but it does when a subordinate does not take care of the troops.

CHAPTER 9

Stress Management

More study and reading convinced me that we must do something about the stress associated with being a DI. Too many good NCOs were being ruined, and I felt that we could do more to relieve the situation. We had a program at our Family Services Center dealing with the DIs and family problems. It was operated by Dr. Neidig, a PhD from town, and he seemed to know what he was doing. I asked him to come by my office and gave him copies of the studies conducted at San Diego. I said, "I want to prevent the DIs from getting into trouble, and I believe that you may be able to help. Would you study these reports and then tell me what you think." In the meantime, I contacted the navy psychologists at the clinic and gave them the same instructions and asked them to come up with a program that could be used for those DIs approaching the one-year period so perhaps we could prevent disasters from happening rather than dealing with them after they occurred. They returned a week or so later and outlined a program for DIs prior to the one-year period. We gathered all the first sergeants and senior gunnery sergeants who had a prior tour as DIs and used them as guinea pigs. We then adjusted the program and required all DIs with ten to fourteen months on the field to attend.

Diary, March 17, 1983.

> *The stress management classes started yesterday for the DIs. Dr. Howell is really enthused.*

The psychologists developed a four—to six-hour presentation of lectures and discussions with small groups of DIs. I preceded each class with a short introduction outlining why I thought it so important to take DIs away from their platoons for these periods.

I assured them that their best interest was at heart, and then I left.

Shortly after this started, the family services center informed me that it had some money to spend on the DIs and their families. It was determined that this money could be used for stress management classes, and a contract was drawn up and opened for bids. Since I had a definite interest and knew that Dr. Neidig probably would be submitting a bid, I disqualified myself from sitting on the board. It made no difference because he won the contract anyway.

That program consisted of a ten-hour course, two hours a week for five weeks. It addressed the causes of stress, its effects on the family, its effect on work, how to reduce it, how to recognize it, and how to manage it. It included homework, self-tests, and the reading of blood pressure and pulse rates. The classes consisted of groups with either ten DIs or officers and their wives. By the end of the contract, 315 DIs, 43 officers, and 47 wives had attended. Once again, I preceded each class with a short introduction.

Throughout the entire time that this was done, the biggest complaint by the DIs was stress management classes. They fought tooth and nail, but it was done, and the results spoke for themselves. That, combined with many other changes, resulted in a reduction of recruit abuse by over 67 percent. Fewer DIs were finding themselves in trouble, and the recruits were being trained better.

Months later, I had numerous DIs tell me that they had not fully understood the rationale behind the training but that they thought that it was very beneficial. Their wives told my wife that they could see the difference in their husbands. They wanted to know why we did not continue the program.

We were convinced that the program was effective even before we could fully analyze the data.

Diary, February 25, 1984

> *Met with Dr. Neidig. The data is indisputable. It works! We can devise an instrument to predict. The change in DIs is dramatic, and we can adjust the program to deal with bachelors.*

The change in attitudes and perceptions from pre- and post-testing left little doubt. The most encouraging aspect was that those DIs who needed to change the most actually changed the most.

Headquarters was informed, and a request to continue the program was submitted. Unfortunately, it was not met with the same enthusiasm, and we were told to stop until further study could be conducted.

Our hands were tied. I called headquarters and spoke to the staff officer responsible and was informed that he was looking at it. No more classes were held while I was in the Regiment.

One of the side benefits surfaced with the officers, for many of them also were required to attend. They became more aware of the telltale signs of stress and prevented many DIs from ruining themselves by getting them away from the recruits before it was too late.

The symptoms were evident if one watched and studied the men. I recall on one occasion when I observed a DI who had been in minor trouble in the past. He was a bachelor, a PT fanatic from a technical MOS, and approaching one year on the field. All of that could add up to trouble.

He seemed to be on edge, and I passed the word to the battalion commander to have him transferred to Support Battalion for a short rest.

The following Saturday, I noticed him still with his platoon. I went to the battalion to speak to the commanding officer (CO), but he was elsewhere, and his executive officer (XO) informed me that the CO did not agree with me and wanted to discuss the matter. Presently, the CO arrived and we spoke. He wanted to keep the DI until the platoon graduated, which did not occur for seven weeks. I said, "No, he will never make it, move him." The CO then asked if he could keep him at least until the following Friday so that he could better adjust in shifting DIs. I thought for a moment and gave the approval.

The following Wednesday, that CO came to see me and said that he had to relieve that particular DI. I did not bother to say "I told you so." It was not necessary.

Later in the week, I spoke to that particular DI and asked him if he could explain why he had difficulties. He could not tell me exactly why, but at the same time he said that he desired to change and didn't know how to go about it. I made arrangements for him to see one of the civilian psychologists at family services that happened to be the wife of one of the doctors. She and I talked about this particular DI, and she started to meet with him. A week or so after his meetings with her, I spoke to him again and asked if it had helped. He could not have spoken more highly about her or about his new outlook. I asked him if he would share some of his new feelings with his fellow DIs and perhaps we could convince some of them that the psychologists were on our side.

I said that because I had read the congressional hearings from 1976, and some of the most damaging testimony came from the psychologists who usually saw only those recruits who were having difficulties in adjusting to military life. None of them either took or were given the opportunity to see other than problem recruits. Naturally, their opinions of recruits and DIs were skewed. In an attempt to correct that, I encouraged the psychologists to visit the training of platoons so that they would not become disillusioned and they could see firsthand what we were trying to do. Periodically, I checked to see if, in fact, they were visiting the field. Their attitudes also changed as they saw what we were trying to do and that most of the recruits were really fantastic young men. An interesting aspect of this approach is that it can be used in other areas where individuals are under significant stress such as the police or prisons.

CHAPTER 10

Stories

After being in the Regiment for a while, I made it a point to learn the names of the DIs and took great pleasure in coming up behind one of them and calling him by name. They thought that the colonel was only supposed to know the names of those in trouble, and I knew that it would get their attention. As the old saying goes, nothing sounds sweeter to an individual than his own name. The sergeant major went with me on all my tours, and I used his expertise to learn the names of most of the DIs. In the process, I became very familiar with their capabilities and began to predict who would win the final drill before they ever drilled. It was not that difficult after observing the senior DI, the experienced DI, how they worked together, and how they treated their recruits. I also would watch the recruits drilling to determine if any one platoon had more than its share of recruits with two left feet. No matter how good a DI was, he could not win the final drill if he did not have his share of coordinated recruits. The recruits actually won the drill, although the senior DI could lose it by not being sharp. I would arrive at the competition and ask the series officer who he thought would win and then write on a piece of paper my prediction and tell him to place it in his pocket until after the last platoon drilled. I was correct 90 percent of the time.

One day we were all standing around waiting for the start of the final PFT, and the senior DIs were working with their platoons. The series officer and I were discussing the final drill scheduled for the following day, and I asked him who he thought would win. As it turned out, the platoon that he predicted was in front of us and the DI was giving it hell. As it practiced movements, the DI really raised hell and told the recruits that they did not want to win.

He berated them for not trying hard enough and not paying attention. They became more hesitant with their responses as they attempted to refrain from making mistakes. The platoon became worse rather than better. The DI was attempting to motivate the recruits, but he went too far. Rather than motivate them, he convinced them that they could not win. I turned to the series officer and said, "I'm not sure at the moment who will win, but I know who will not." He asked why, and I explained my reasoning. I had observed that particular series frequently during drill, and the platoons were closely matched. The following day I told him that Staff Sergeant Glick, the senior DI from another platoon, would win, and he did. The DI who had been berating his platoon came in last.

Recruit Competence

During one of the fireside chats, the competence of the recruits came up, and the DIs said that they did not perform up to their capabilities. They felt that they did not put out 100 percent. In their minds, the recruits should be fully capable of performing as well as the DIs. That was totally unrealistic. I thought for a moment and then started. "Let's say that we are going to bake a cake. We mix the ingredients together and then preheat the oven to the proper temperature. We place the cake into the oven for the required amount of time, and we have a cake. Now suppose that we become impatient. If we turn the heat up, the cake will not bake faster, but rather, it will burn. The exact same thing happens to the recruits. At the present time, it takes fifty-six training days to make a Marine, and if we attempt to rush the process, the product can be spoiled. The recruits will not be in as good shape at the initial PFT as they will at the final one, they will not march as well at the initial drill as at the final drill, they will not know as much in phase 1 as in phase 3. I repeat, it takes 56 days to make a Marine." I always tried to use an analogy to drive my points across, but I'm sure that many of the DIs thought that it might be good for baking a cake but not training a recruit.

IPT

Incentive Physical Training (IPT) managed to keep many DIs in trouble. They desired to have more of it, and I thought that too frequently it was nonproductive. They would do it at the wrong time or do too much of it. "Sir, we must be allowed to discipline the recruits." What they meant was that they wanted to wear them out. My response was that IPT did not have that as its purpose. The maximum amount of time that a DI could IPT a recruit was five minutes, two and one half minutes with a half-minute rest followed by another two and one half minutes. "Let me tell you the purpose for IPT. You want the recruit to know that you know that he is not performing up to standards. You also want the platoon to know that you know that he is not performing up to standards, and you want to embarrass him—not humiliate but embarrass. You cannot wear a recruit out with IPT, and you cannot get him in shape with it. If you try, you will be in trouble. After you complete the required IPT and then the recruit smiles, you will make him do additional exercises. He will do it, but he now has a bright shiny dime, which he can drop on you at any time because he knows that you have disobeyed orders. Wouldn't it be better to have him do a few mountain climbers and push-ups and then return to ranks? You will have accomplished all the goals. If at a later time he fouls up again, you do it a little longer until finally you are at the maximum time of five minutes. Why start with the maximum when it may not be necessary? It's like my holding office hours (nonjudicial punishment, the military equivalent of a court hearing.) Although I have the capability to take a stripe, one half of one month's pay for two months and restriction and extra duty for forty-five days, that normally does not happen the first time unless it is a relatively serious offense.

I try to give myself maneuver room and look at each case individually. Not all cases require the maximum punishment, and if they did, why bother with office hours? The same applies for IPT."

First Sergeant Moore
Diary, January 20, 1983

Talked (rather listened to) 1st Sgt. Moore and left there on cloud nine. IF all DIs thought that way there would be no problems.

First Sergeant Moore shared with me his thoughts on IPT and why he thought that it became a constant problem. He said, "Colonel, did you ever notice that the average officer with ten or more years in the Corps generally looks pretty good and keeps himself in good shape? Many of the average enlisted men are not the same. I believe that much of it is caused by attitude. Each time that we desire to gain the attention of an enlisted man, we PT him. PT for him becomes a negative influence, and we normally do not seek out negatives. The officers look at PT from a positive viewpoint and the good that it accomplishes. It may sound simple, but it sure does make sense to me." Once again, this superb SNCO spoke words of wisdom. Too frequently, we never take the time to analyze exactly why we do certain things and determine if there is, perhaps, a better method. First Sergeant Moore was a thinker.

Giving the DIs a Break

Although the manning level of the Regiment calls for almost six hundred DIs, there are times, because of the number of recruits aboard and the DIs assigned, when it is necessary to have DIs work back to back with platoons. That means that some of the DIs must start a new platoon as soon as they graduate the old one. That can be disastrous if it is not absolutely necessary. The DIs need a break after graduating a platoon. That allows them to forget about their present platoon and merely relax. If there is no break, it is difficult to adjust to a new platoon that does not know anything about drill or any of the other routines. The DI may forget that it is new and think that it just does not care. He may then become frustrated and resort to other tactics. After eleven weeks of being with a platoon and teaching the entire time, they are worn out. S. L. A. Marshall, a noted military author, touched on fatigue in many of his writings concerning combat and combat fatigue. He felt that many good men could be returned to duty following a break from combat and its effects and become as effective as they were originally. I used that philosophy in Vietnam, and I felt the same about the DIs wearing themselves out. The DIs themselves did not fully appreciate how much of a toll was extracted by being with a platoon constantly for eleven weeks. They felt that it was their job and that they could go on forever. Dedication is good, and it contributed to the competence of the DIs, but when allowed to be carried to extremes, it did more harm than good. I demanded that the DIs be given three days off with no duties whatsoever following the graduation of his platoon. He could not be assigned to the rifle range or any other type of duty during this time.

The Slow March

The normal speed for marching is "quick time," which is 120 steps per minute. When initially teaching drill, it is taught by the numbers. Each movement takes from two to five steps. When doing it by the numbers, only one step at a time is completed and corrected before the next step is commenced. Over the years, that evolved into the slow march at Parris Island. Rather than stop at each count, the platoon moved at slow motion. It was not unusual to see a platoon marching at about sixty steps per minute. The DIs explained that it was easier to teach at that speed and that the speed would eventually increase to 120.

In many cases, the DIs used the slow march during Phase III to embarrass their platoon in front of other platoons. I failed to see the reasoning for teaching something wrong and then somehow or other expecting it to develop into the correct result. Actually, it was rather amusing at times to see the recruits moving so slowly, but it was counterproductive. One of the battalion commanders told me that there would be a mutiny if I tried to change it. It was not high on the hit parade, so it remained for about a year. Then it too was changed without too much fuss.

Time Management and Shining Gear

One of the major complaints of the DIs was that there wasn't enough time to teach all that was required. They constantly looked for shortcuts. In the operating forces there are very few Marines who shine leather shoes or regular brass. We discovered fantastic substitutes, corfam shoes and anodized brass. I authorized their use in Boot Camp, and one would have thought that I had destroyed the Corps. How could I have done such a thing? Marines must shine their shoes! They must shine their brass! Almost all DIs and officers used these easier techniques themselves. However, one could not allow the recruits to do it. That violated tradition. "Sir, it's tradition!" They could not see that it gave them more time to spend on the important areas where there were no easier methods. We do not have a self-cleaning rifle or the ability to take a pill for knowledge. It must be done the hard way. Why not take advantage of the easier method where appropriate? The purpose of shining shoes and brass is to make them look good, and if there is an easier method, use it.

Spend some initial time to teach them how to do it and then move on to other more important areas. Years ago, we spent much more time doing mundane things, and much of it was merely to keep the troops busy. We didn't make much money, and the weapons were much simpler, so time was available to do these things. We no longer have that luxury. More time must be spent with complicated weapons and how to operate them. We can capture that time by training smarter. When I was at Marine Barracks in Washington, DC, the troops and officers spent untold hours daily shining items because at that time there was no substitute.

Recruit Wrap

Everyone knows about loneliness, and everyone has experienced it at one time or another. Christmas is one of those special times when families get together and share in the joy of being a family. Being separated at that particular time is bad enough, but being in Boot Camp can make it even worse. Several years ago, someone at the depot decided to do something about it and started a program, Recruit Wrap.

All the recruits who had been in training for a couple of weeks and would not be home for Christmas were given a special advance pay and, on various evenings, marched to the Post Exchange (PX) for the opportunity to buy gifts for family and friends. They were then taken to the gym where all their gifts were wrapped and from there to the post office where they were mailed. The organization and support for this was extensive and involved much of the depot. Thirty to fifty women had to be available each night for wrapping presents. The PX officer and personal services officer coordinated to have boxes, wrapping paper, bows, etc., available for about twelve nights. The logistics for the entire affair was fascinating and, at times, frustrating. How do you convince a mother and wife that she should come to Recruit Wrap at dinnertime and possibly remain until 2300?

The responsibility for those tasks fell to my wife, Grace. She was super! Her part of the task went like clockwork.

The first year that I became involved with this, I was told that the DIs would not be allowed to enter the area where the recruits had their gifts wrapped because they made the recruits nervous. Bull! The recruits were the responsibility of the DIs, and they would go wherever the recruits went.

Each night for twelve nights, Grace and I met at the Recruit Wrap. We compared notes and roared. Several of the daughters of the officers helped, and if I do say so myself, they were good-looking. They did not go unnoticed by the recruits, and on one occasion, they were overheard to be talking about them. One recruit asked, "Do you think that they are daughters of the DIs?" Another recruit responded without any malice, "No, they are too good-looking to be their daughters."

Grace came home one night chuckling about one of the recruits. The young man approached her, and she started to speak in a cheery tone with much animation as is her usual custom. The recruit looked relieved and said, "Thank God you are in a good mood, I've been dealing with nothing but sourpusses all day!" She almost cracked up and was still laughing when she came in the door.

Trust

Prior to my arriving in the Regiment, one of the DIs was court-martialed for ordering his recruit billet holders to "square away" other recruits. In the eyes of the recruits, that meant to beat them, and they complied. In this particular case, it had occurred at Page Field. They had taken one of the recruits into the woods, and as he performed push-ups, they started to kick him.

Fortunately, other recruits from another series interfered, and the beating stopped before they had done permanent damage. As it was, he required hospitalization and his face was a mess.

At the court-martial, one of the assistant DIs presented damaging evidence. He had since been discharged and testified as a civilian. In order to impeach the witness, the defense brought forth other witnesses—the company commander, series commander, and first sergeant of the company. Each person was asked if they knew the former Marine. They replied yes. They then were asked if they would believe his sworn testimony. They all said that they would not believe him if he had sworn on a stack of bibles, because he could not be trusted. As I read the record of trial, I found it difficult to control myself. Here we had the top leadership of a company who all agreed that a particular DI was untrustworthy, and yet they had entrusted a platoon of recruits to his care. I immediately called for the battalion commanders, and when they arrived, I outlined the story for them. Then I continued, "This happened prior to my arrival, but I want to be assured that there are no DIs in any of your units whom you do not trust. If there is anyone who you do not fully trust, then I want his hat. I will not jeopardize the Corps for the sake of an individual who thinks that he can make a Marine his way." Each, in turn, assured me that that was not the case. They trusted all their DIs, and that's the way it should be.

The Old Corps

One afternoon as I departed the First Battalion's mess hall, I bumped into a middle-aged man who asked about the series that was due to graduate the following morning. As it turned out, the series was in Company A, and I pointed out the location to him. He had a nephew in the series, and it was obvious that he was extremely proud. He continued to linger, and it also was obvious that he wanted to talk. After making small talk and talking about the base and the weather, he stated that he had graduated from PI in the '50s. He spoke about the Corps and finally said, "I sure hope that you still train 'em like you used to." Without any hesitation, I replied, "I sure hope that we don't." He looked puzzled, and I continued to speak about how we trained them now and the results of it on the operating forces. In astonishment, he asked, "How can you instill discipline if the DIs can't lay hands on the recruits?" We spoke for well over an hour about the training, the quality of recruits, and many other subjects. I asked him about the type of leadership that he encountered following Boot Camp. He spoke very highly about it and agreed that his NCOs in the operating forces treated him fairly but firmly. Before he left to search out his nephew, we shook hands and he said, "You really believe everything that you said, don't you?" "Ask your nephew what he thought of the training, and I'm sure that he will say that it was tough. We train smart, not easy, and abuse is not necessary."

The Range Officer and Discipline

The range officer stood at the center of the line as the recruits fired at their targets and attempted to qualify with the M16s. It was quite obvious that he was not too happy with the proceedings. I approached him and asked, "Well, gunner (warrant officer), what do you think of these new recruits?" I had known the gunner when he was a gunnery sergeant in the Second Marines a year or so earlier and knew that he had been a DI during the '70s. He had been a no-nonsense NCO who got results. "They are smart, sir, but they are undisciplined and ask too many questions," he responded. "What makes you say that they are undisciplined?" "Sir, they want to know the answer to everything, and they talk back. Let me give you an example. I told the line NCO that we had a problem with marking the targets, and we went to a recruit who was sitting on the ready box. I told him to mark the target." He looked at me and said, "Sir, the target doesn't need to be marked." As I prepared to respond, I had to chuckle to myself, because he had just described a recruit who had used his initiative and the reason we will beat any enemy if it becomes necessary.

At the rifle range, there are fifty targets on each range with a firing position for each target. Behind each firing position, there is a white ammo box on which the recruit scheduled to fire next sits. At the center of the line is a tower with the line NCO who has communications with the butts where the targets are located. Whenever any target is fired upon and the target is not pulled for marking, the line NCO calls the butts. When a recruit fires and his target is not marked, the recruit on the ready box stands up and places his inboard foot on the box. That indicates to the line NCO that the target needs to be checked for a bullet hole, and he informs the butts. On the side of each box facing the tower is the number of that specific target.

Apparently what had been happening was that some of the recruits had been placing the wrong foot on the box, and their other leg had been hiding the number. When the warrant officer told the recruit to "mark your target," the recruit knew that it had not been fired upon, and if it were pulled, it would be recorded as a miss. He probably thought that the gunner had seen someone else shoot and had confused the numbers. In his mind, it was a stupid and wrong order, and he was attempting to prevent an error from being made. I explained this to the gunner, but he felt that it made no difference. Since he was a warrant officer, the recruit should have obeyed even if he knew that it was wrong. I said, "Gunner, if you had said, 'Recruit, show me how you would call for a mark,' he would have done it because it made sense." The gunner persisted in his assertions. "Sir, in combat, when they are told to keep their heads down, they will want to know why and get killed as a result." I continued to press the point. "You are wrong, gunner. Let me explain why. You must develop a sense of trust among your subordinates by explaining your actions. When the occasion arrives and there is no time to explain, they will respond because of that trust, and the fact that they know you will explain your actions later. We do not need robots because our next enemy will probably have more than we. The only way that we can win the next war is to be better. We must be able to think and not just blindly follow. Do you understand the difference?" He didn't. In his mind, he was senior and all orders should be obeyed immediately with no thinking possible. There was no sense trying to push it any further that day. There would be other days.

The Turning Point

The commanding general and I spoke about training recruits almost every day. I outlined all the plans as they were formulated and emphasized that the key element was the changing of attitudes. His total support was heartwarming. We spoke often about the proper training of recruits and the role of leadership. At one of these meetings, I predicted that once we had a handle on the problem of recruit abuse, it would go down and stay down. There would be times when, for whatever reason, there would be a bubble, but the incidents would remain low.

Diary, January 11, 1983

The recruit information system <RIS> for DEC. was low again "3." We had "2" for Nov.

The RIS was a report, which each depot sent to headquarters monthly indicating the number of allegations against DIs and their outcome. The turning point occurred in November 1982. After six months of talking, explaining, observing, and walking around the Regiment, the report showed a definite drop in incidents. We were winning! At every opportunity, I spoke to officers and DIs and congratulated them on their performance. They were producing good Marines, and they were doing it within the prescribed parameters, and the DIs were not getting into trouble.

Diary, December 6, 1982

We are in the fourth week of no DIs pending a court for recruit abuse. That's fantastic!

The Talk to the Honor Graduates

As each series was scheduled to graduate, I spoke to the platoon honor graduates in my office two or three days before the event. The following is generally what I said: "You are about to become full-fledged members of the finest military organization in the world—the Marines. That is not because I say so, but rather, the record speaks for itself. For more than two hundred years, we have been serving the country and doing it well. Although we are small when compared to the other services, we are one of the largest armies in the world. We are larger than the army of England, we are larger than the entire armed forces of Canada, and our air component is one of the largest in the world. It hasn't always been super. We have had a few rough years. The most recent was in the early and mid '70s. We had just come out of Vietnam, and the draft was coming to an end. Our end strength was much larger than now, and we desired to keep it above two hundred thousand. Unfortunately, we were unable to recruit the numbers of quality men to do this and we lowered standards to meet the numbers.

That, along with social problems in our society, caused problems in our Corps. There were race riots, drugs, murders, and all sorts of other crime on most of our major bases. Boot Camp at that time was brutal, and in the words of General Barrow, our commandant, it was institutionalized. There were many reasons for it, but ultimately there was no excuse. If brutality developed discipline, then why was the lack of discipline so prevalent in the '70s?

"The two most important things that we attempt to do in Boot Camp are to develop and instill pride and discipline. They cannot be taught, they must be developed. If anyone could design a course that taught them, he would be an instant millionaire. It must be done by example, and by doing all those good things dealing with leadership and not merely talking about them.

"It is less than effective to tell recruits that Marines do not lie, steal, or cheat and then have a recruit take a test for a slower recruit. Our actions speak louder than our words. How can one cheat and expect to teach honesty, how can one disobey orders and expect to teach respect for orders, how can one lie and expect to teach integrity? It cannot be done!

"We are a band of brothers in every sense of the word. As an organization, we care about what happens to you and to your family. We will go out of our way to assist you, but you must let us know if there is a problem. You will find that being a Marine is fun. Why else would so many of us remain for a career? I can assure you that it isn't for the money, although the pay is not bad. We remain because it's fun. I will guarantee that you will have some bad days along the way, but for the most part, you will remember them in jest. The lingering memories will be the good times and friends that you will keep for a lifetime.

"Let me change the subject and discuss you and your performance. You have broken the code! Within the next couple of days, you will dramatically see that the Corps rewards good performance. Promotions, assignments, pay, letters, citations, and medals are all provided to those who perform well. We like to think that all Marines are super, but some are still better than others.

"The top ones are recognized. You can look better than most people with extra effort, but to be in the very top, you must be better. On the other side of the coin, the Corps becomes quite upset with those who do not meet the standards. You have heard many people, including the commanding general, speak about the abuse of drugs. We fully intend to rid our ranks of those who use them. The bottom line is that we must be ready to go to war, and an individual who uses drugs is a risk. It would be bad enough for him to get himself killed, but we sure don't want him to get good Marines killed. Anyone who uses drugs is a quitter. He is trying to escape from a problem rather than solve it. Since we decided to rid our ranks of drug abusers in late 1981, our disciplinary problems have continued to go down each year.

"That's enough of that. Now let me hear what you have to say about the training, which you received. What was the most difficult part of

Boot Camp?" The answer to that question varied, but it amazed me at how many felt that *forming* was the most difficult. Other areas that came up were the PT, field training, gas chamber, and mess duty.

The next question that I asked was for the easiest part of training. Many felt that no part of it was easy. In their minds, it was all difficult. However, the areas that did arise were the rifle range, PT, and academics. The final area that we discussed was change. What would you change in Boot Camp? The greatest percentage said nothing; however, some asked for more PT, fieldwork, and shooting.

More often than not, the recruits needed little encouragement to talk or ask questions.

They appeared to be rather eager to see the Corps following Boot Camp. A later assignment following Parris Island allowed me to see these young men as Marines, and I could not have been more pleased with how they performed both on and off duty.

Flag Conditions

The heat at Parris Island can become stifling during the summer, but then it is no worse than that found in many other parts of the world where we might be required to fight. While talking to a group of DIs outside of the classroom as the recruits took their Phase I tests, one of the DIs suggested that we should do away with the flag conditions for training.

We normally restricted certain levels of training during extreme heat, and to indicate the levels of heat, a different colored flag was flown from various poles throughout the depot. His point was that there were no flag conditions during combat. He wore a few rows of ribbons from Vietnam, so it was obvious that he had served there. That, in and of itself, made no one an expert on training or combat, and so I decided to make a point. "Gunny, how much walking did you do in Vietnam?" I asked. He responded that he had been in the artillery and they rode most of the time. I continued, "I agree that there are no flag conditions in combat, but I can assure you that I spent two tours in the infantry in combat and we did a lot of walking. We also paid attention to the heat. Anyone who failed to pay attention paid a great price in heat casualties. It made no difference to me if one of my Marines was wounded or extracted because of heat. He was still gone, and I could not use him. When the heat was at its worst, we slowed down, drank more water, and the casualties reflected it. We took few heat casualties, and we were very successful. That speaks for combat and for the training here. We cannot train a recruit if he is dead from heat stroke or if he is taken to the dispensary because of heat exhaustion. We don't train easy, we train smart. Even when I advised a Vietnamese infantry battalion, they paid attention to the heat. Why do you think that most countries in the Southern Hemisphere take a siesta during the noon hour? That's when it is the hottest." We spoke a little more, and he could see the reasoning behind my rationale.

New Officers

As each new officer arrived in the Regiment, I spoke with him for about two hours. I outlined my philosophy of leadership and the history of recruit training to include the difficulties that had been experienced in the past.

I stressed that his duties did not include training the recruits. That belonged to the DIs. He was there to lead DIs and ensure that the recruits were trained properly. He would be attending a two-week series officer school, which would cover all aspects of recruit training with emphasis on the SOP.

One of the final things that I spoke of was the dealings with the DIs. "It must not be an adversary relationship but, rather, a partnership. You must know the SOP thoroughly. We have made great strides in the changing of attitudes, but there is much work to be done! The DIs are among the finest NCOs that you will ever see, but we still have some hard noses who insist on training recruits their way. At the very minimum, if you see or hear a DI do something that he is not supposed to do, you must say something. More often than not, he didn't know that it was wrong, however, he could be one of the hard noses who is just checking you out. If that is the case, he will do something that is rather minor to determine your reaction. If you say nothing, he will probably do it again and then do something more serious and continue until finally you must say something. At that time he will probably say, 'Sir, I don't understand. Yesterday when I did such and such you said nothing, and I assumed that you felt that it was no big deal, and now you say it is.' He is telling you that you allowed him to violate orders and said nothing. He now has a bright, shiny dime in his pocket, which he can drop on you at any time, and you had better leave him alone. You have been compromised!"

Summer and Winter Recruits

Since the Corps looks for high school graduates and they do graduate in the summer, a large percentage of them attend Boot Camp at that time, and the recruit load is always much larger in the summer than the winter. In the recent past, that resulted in a difference between summer and winter platoons. The summer platoons were generally smarter and had more education than the winter platoons. As a result, the DIs expected different results from each and handled them a little differently. There were two schools of thought on the subject. Some DIs preferred the winter platoons because they felt that they asked fewer questions and were more motivated than the smarter summer ones. Other DIs felt that the winter platoons were rocks and that resulted in their spending more time explaining all aspects of training, but at least they asked no questions.

As I looked at the statistics of the incoming winter platoons, it became obvious that it no longer held true. Recruiters had been doing such a good job that many of the recruits who graduated from high school in the summer could not be shipped to PI because there was no room. We placed them in a delayed entry program to await shipping to PI when there was room. For many of them, that was the winter. If the DIs had a preconceived notion of what to expect, they could run into difficulties. I started to talk to many DIs and stress this fact. In addition, I mentioned it in my weekly paper, the *Word*:

> Winter Recruits
> Many of them enlisted months earlier and could not start Boot Camp until now. They may be totally different than previous "winter" recruits.

The Colonel's Aide

Attempting to change attitudes and perceptions can be a very time-consuming and frustrating job. Each of the battalions had a very definite personality, and naturally, they felt that they did everything better than anyone else. One day, I decided to try a different tack in convincing certain DIs that there was more than one way to skin a cat. I would have a DI report to my office, and for about three days, he went everywhere I went so he could see for himself what the entire Regiment was doing and listen to the sergeant major and me talk and see what we looked for. It also gave him the opportunity to offer his observations and comments.

Diary, May 2, 1983

Started taking SSgt. Dinkel around with me last Thursday. He has had a few surprises because it is not quite as he thought. Apparently the battalion is really talking about it.

When the DI initially arrived, he was almost in a panic because nothing had been explained except that he was to report to the Colonel. After putting his mind at ease, we would start, and like everything else, it developed a name—the Colonel's Aide. The sergeant major was the first one to hear that and clue me in. I didn't care what they called it as long as they got something out of it.

Private Jones

On one of my evening tours through the Regiment, I walked into a squad bay, and one of the DIs was really raising hell with a recruit. The rest of the platoon had prepared for showers and was rapidly moving into the head. This particular recruit had just completed some IPT and then moved toward his rack to get his clothes off for a shower. I asked the DI about the recruit, and he said that he was belligerent. In the meantime, the recruit at the end of the squad bay could be heard huffing and puffing. The DI said, "Sir, he always has to get in the last word." I asked about his background, such as education and number of brothers and sisters. The DI was not sure since the platoon was on about training day 7. I walked to the end of the squad bay and met Private Jones, who was eighteen years old. He had stripped to his shorts, and it was obvious that he had good muscle tone. It also was obvious that his lower jaw protruded such that his face always presented a scowl, which would give the appearance of belligerence. I asked if he had any trouble with PT and he responded, "No, sir." I then asked if he had any brothers and sisters, and he replied that he had three sisters. He stated that he was the youngest. I then asked what the problem was. He stood about five feet, ten inches and weighed about 160 pounds. He really looked like a good recruit. He could hardly contain his frustration as he started to explain. "Sir, the private never seems to be able to please the DIs. No matter what I do, it is always wrong. They never seem to let up on me."

"Let me tell you something, Jones. I am sure that as you grew up, your sisters paid a lot of attention to you, and when they didn't, you acted out and then received it. That was very successful for you, and I suspect that you are trying the same thing here. I guarantee that if you act out here, the DIs will also give you attention, but it will not be the kind that you desire. They have your number right now, and you must get off the skyline. What you want to do is listen to everything that they say and do it as rapidly as you possibly can. As soon as you show them that you will respond, they will get off of your case. Try it and see what happens."

During grass week at the rifle range, which was about three weeks later, I saw Private Jones in his PT gear with the rest of the platoon and spoke to the DI. "How's Private Jones doing?" "Great," he replied. I then went over to Jones and called him by his name. He appeared surprised since his name was not written anywhere. I said, "Jones, do you remember our talk?" He said, "Yes, sir." "Did it work?" "Yes, sir." "Hang in there, son." It sure does give one a good feeling when you win one.

The Recruits Speak

The honor graduates of each platoon came to my office prior to graduation, and we talked for quite some time. At one of these talks, one of the recruits asked about the DIs. He had a year of college and was a good-looking young man with quite a grasp of the language. He said, "Sir, why is it that the DIs rant and rave and scream and shout for fifteen minutes, and after they are through, we still don't know what they want us to do? If they would just tell us, we would do it." I had to giggle. "Son, you are singing my song," I told him.

Giving 100 Percent

No one could ever accuse the DIs of not asking for the maximum effort from the recruits at all times. Normally, they asked too much, and it was difficult to convince them otherwise. One day, I thought of the following analogy and used it on the DIs in an attempt to convince them to use the best judgment possible. "The recruits are afraid to give 100 percent because of what happens later. Let me give you an example of what I mean. Suppose I take all of you outside and tell you that I want you to run three miles as fast as you can. As soon as you complete it, I tell you that you must run another three miles, and if you cannot run it at the same speed, then there will be no time off this weekend. If you really ran that first three miles as fast as you could, then it is unlikely that you could match it immediately.

"Tomorrow, I take all of you outside again and tell you to run three miles as fast as you can. As soon as you complete it, I tell you to run another three miles, and if you cannot run it at the same speed, then no time off next weekend. The following day, we go through the same routine. By this time, you are smart, and you run the first three miles at the speed that you feel that you can run the following three miles. You have already lost two weekends of liberty and you are not about to lose another one.

"The recruits do the same thing. You ask them for 100 percent. They give it, and then you ask for more and there is nothing left. Then they are punished. They are fast learners, and after being caught once or twice, they always keep a little in reserve for what they know will follow. I am not preaching the lowering of standards but, rather, being reasonable. When they give 100 percent, be satisfied at that particular time, and then raise the standard later."

Reveille to Taps

When a new DI arrived in his first platoon, the senior DI used many different techniques to prepare him to be an effective member of the team. One of those methods was "reveille to taps." The new man was required to be with the platoon during the entire day in an effort to learn as much as possible in a short time. On the surface, that is rather smart, but after a few days of this, the new DI can literally wear himself out. By the time that he drives home, prepares his gear for the following day, and goes to bed, he may be getting just a couple of hours' sleep. After many days of this, he is falling asleep in the mashed potatoes at home and not learning too much of anything. Some of the seniors felt obligated to keep a new man on this routine for a couple of weeks. They failed to realize that it could very easily be doing the opposite of what they wanted. Fatigue slows the learning process and contributes to poor judgment. Some felt that it made a better DI if he could stand the pressure of this. My answer was that we already had enough pressure and stress without manufacturing additional elements. I did not want reveille to taps to last longer than two or three days and then give the DI a break to have his batteries recharged without being around the recruits.

CHAPTER 11

Goals

Most of the adjustments at Parris Island did not occur as a result of a brainstorm but after careful observation and thought. As mentioned earlier, it has been my habit for more than twenty years to keep a diary, especially in combat or command. Parris Island was no exception. The blue notebook went everywhere with me as I kept notes on meetings or observations. I'm sure that there was many a joke about the colonel and his notebook. (Years later when I attended a reunion with the DIs, the matter of the blue notebook surfaced and I read excerpts from it.)

In order to ensure that none of the elements or units in the Regiment or depot were overlooked in my travels, I made a list of them all and religiously noted on that list those elements, which I visited each day. I recorded when, where, and the action taking place. By the time that I left the Regiment, I was visiting each series between forty to fifty times before it graduated. All other elements such as depot, supply, inspectors, admin, classroom, swimming, rifle range, mess halls, etc., were visited at least once a week, and the more significant ones at least every third day. I was in the mess halls nearly every day. In that manner, the lines of communication remained as open as I could make them, and we did not surprise each other. If for any reason I had not seen a series for three days, I deliberately went looking for it. The DIs and officers always knew that I would be around to talk and listen. After a while they began to tell me more about the various things that bothered them.

The missions of the Recruit Training Regiment are spelled out in orders; however, there are numerous methods to attain them. It has been my habit to establish goals as I went along. This assignment was no different. Although I had no preconceived notions before I arrived, I started developing goals almost immediately. From my viewpoint, that is only the first step. Next, one must inform others about those goals and ensure that they are shared. I started to publish a one-page paper each Friday, the *Word*, so that I could talk to all hands and allow them to see where we were going and why. The following is an example of the first *Word* that I published.

January 7, 1983
And the Word Is—

Over the last several months, it has become obvious that all the members of the Regiment do not receive the word. Starting this week, I will publish each Friday a one page sheet in an attempt to dispel rumors and ensure that all hands are informed of what is happening in the Regiment and why.

Recruit Load—Unless the Corps decides to increase end strength, there will be a max of 24 series this summer.

Quality—The CG has established a goal of 90% high school graduates for recruit input this year.

We must continue to remind ourselves that the mission of the Regiment is to train a Basic Marine, not a combat Marine.

Parade Deck—The reviewing stands will be rebuilt starting on 17 Jan. That will require several months, but the ceremony will remain the same.

Winter Recruits—Many of them enlisted months ago and could not start Boot Camp until now. They may be totally different than previous "winter" recruits.

The battalions have been authorized to allow the recruits to purchase anodized brass. The recruit PX will have it in stock within weeks.

The IG inspection is approaching. Ensure that all of your uniforms are serviceable and fit properly. There will be preliminary inspections, but they should not interfere with recruit training.

We have made some fine tuning adjustments in recruit training over the last several months in an attempt to improve training. That will continue.

EXAMPLES

Swimming S2s have doubled and S3s have increased 10%

ICT Retention of material has improved and the DIs and recruits have more time.

PCP The purpose is to keep a recruit motivated and develop him so that he is in good shape. We are spending less time in PCP and 80% are successfully completing Boot Camp.

RIFLE RANGE Weapons Battalion and the Regiment are working together to ensure that basic marksmanship is being taught. As a result, percentages have gone up.

ITU Many of the classes have been revamped and new training aids made.

PFC We have requested from headquarters an increase in the recruit meritorious promotions from 10% to 15%

Each of these adjustments has come from recommendations within the Regiment. No one has a monopoly on ideas. It is your Regiment and Marine Corps

/s/
D. J. Myers

Many of the good ideas mentioned by the DIs were applauded in the paper as they were implemented. In that way, they received credit and ownership.

By the time that I left the Regiment two years later, the list of goals had grown to over forty with all of them either implemented or underway.

Diary, August 26, 1982

The S4 (Logistics Officer) gave me a briefing on issue of organizational clothing. I think that we can change it, save money for the government, save money for the DIs, and give them a break also. That will be a coup if we can pull it off.

The DIs are required to look sharp at all times, and with only the initial issue of clothing, that is impossible. The Corps issued additional clothing to the DIs so that they would not face undue financial hardships.

Unfortunately, it all was not used. The shirts that we issued were regular cotton, which did not look sharp enough. As a result, the DIs bought creighton shirts, which were very expensive. We changed the issue such that they were issued creighton shirts and additional green trousers and eliminated the issue of leather shoes, which they never wore anyway. In addition, we reduced the issue of camouflage utilities, since they could purchase them inexpensively at clothing issue after they were recovered from recruits who were being sent home. We ended up spending about the same amount of government money, but the DIs spent less of their money and they looked better.

Another challenge existed on the rifle range where the battalions felt compelled to have their DIs qualify with the rifle when their recruits were on mess and maintenance week. In my view, that procedure placed too much pressure on the DIs when they could be relaxing instead. The commanders were told to send the DIs to the range only when they did not have a platoon. If we did not have the opportunity to qualify all the DIs each year, I would take the heat. We normally had enough DIs to accomplish that if the units planned properly.

In order to ensure that the instruction was identical for all recruits and of the same quality, most of the classes were taught by ITU in series-size classrooms. Education should be fun, and that was not always the case, so we revamped the classes and encouraged the instructors to use their imagination. The results paid great dividends as the classes became much more interesting and informative.

The SOP requires all the platoon DIs to be present only four times during the entire training cycle, and yet one would see all the DIs present for duty for nearly every aspect of the training. They felt obligated to be there, and there was an unwritten law that they should be. In a sense, they were wearing themselves out by "kicking rocks." Three DIs were assigned to each platoon so that one could normally be off duty and resting. It would have been easy to put out an order that only those DIs required should be present, but that would not have worked. I tried to show the commanders that it worked contrary to what we wanted to have all the DIs present when it was not necessary. I told them that if they were not required to be there and they could not *add* anything by being there, then don't be there. We put in enough hours without "kicking rocks." It took quite a while, but that too seemed to catch on, and more of the DIs received a break and the needed rest. I recalled being a platoon commander at the Basic School (initial training for new lieutenants), and we were required to be present at all training even when we could not add anything. As a result, we spent untold hours after hours doing necessary paperwork. I did not want the same to be in effect here.

Competition on the field is notorious and did not always contribute to the best interest of the recruits or their development. At times it could become quite cutthroat. That detracted from the mission. The goal should be to produce the best Basic Marine, not to beat another DI. Cooperation was needed among the DIs. How does one encourage cooperation when only winning is rewarded?

Meritorious promotions are the biggest reward in the Regiment, and the letters of recommendations for DI promotions described their performance by the number of events that their platoons won. That caused two problems. First, they felt that they had to win to be promoted, and second, it coerced them to shave corners or cheat. I asked the commanders to submit a word picture of the DI recommended for promotion rather than statistics. Cooperation, motivation, professionalism, bearing, and resourcefulness took on new meanings. In addition, my own observations came into play. I became quite familiar with the capabilities of the DIs and could have written a fitness report on most of them. By the time the records for meritorious promotions reached my desk, they had been through the company, battalion, and Regiment. Almost without exception, I did not agree with all the recommendations and, in each case, would change at least one either to be promoted or not to be promoted. I would normally talk it over with the sergeant major and commanders along with my rationale and then talk directly to the DIs concerned. That method insured that the individuals received the word from the horse's mouth.

After having gone to the Naval Academy, I became quite familiar with sitting at attention during meals as plebes are usually required to do. The only result of that was heartburn. At PI, one could see the recruits also doing this, even though it was against regulations. When I inquired about it, I was told that they merely sat up straight. Bullshit! They sat at attention. In the conversations with the DIs and officers, I used the following analogy: "Let's suppose that you have the finest car in the world that travels at high speeds, rides smoothly, and delivers fantastic mileage. Without gas in the car, it cannot do any of those things except look good. The recruits are the same, and the fuel that they need is food. We must allow them to eat with adequate time and relaxation. Twenty minutes per meal is not asking too much. We work them for sixteen hours a day, and they need all the nourishment that they can receive. I recall from my own experiences in Boot Camp that frequently we were not given time, and somehow, that was supposed to develop discipline. I didn't understand it then, and I don't understand it now."

In the same area, the recruits were discouraged from talking in the mess hall. It was felt that if they were permitted to talk, they would talk each other out of being in Boot Camp. Now came another analogy. "In all my readings of and discussions with our POWs from Vietnam, they seemed to agree on one point. The worst treatment was not the physical torture or poor food but the isolation from other humans and the ability to communicate. They devised elaborate methods to communicate with each other even though discovery meant brutal beatings. The recruits are rather scared and not convinced that they will be able to successfully complete this course, and most of them probably think that they are the only ones who feel that way. If they are allowed to talk, they will discover that they are not alone, and rather than talk each other into leaving, they will talk each other into remaining. Nothing is worse than feeling that you are alone. S. L. A. Marshall, the famous army author, in many of his writings, stressed the need for troops to talk, especially in combat. He felt that it should be stressed from the earliest moment of training. Both of those examples stress the importance of talking, and yet we are deliberately doing the opposite."

Even though we attempted to remain positive and work with all the recruits, there were times when some of them would quit. There also were numerous recruits who had enlisted under fraudulent terms or became injured and required discharge. All those recruits went to the Casual section, where they were separated from the other recruits and processed for discharge. Normal attrition generally hovered around 13 percent.

These particular recruits were the young men who we would be returning to society without becoming Marines. I'm sure that most of them did not have very many good things to say about the Corps, but the last thing that we needed to do was to give them ammunition.

At that particular time, it could take up to two weeks to process all the paperwork for discharge, and in the meantime, we used these recruits for working parties throughout the depot. Many of them had never gone beyond the initial receiving stage while others did not progress beyond

Phase I in the training cycle. They were not going to be Marines, and it made no sense to rag them out. We decided to adjust the procedures at Casual by providing books, games, TV, and motivational talks. We still intended to return them to society better than when they arrived.

I made it a point to talk to many of them during my routine visits, and a sizable number really did not desire to leave. In most of those cases, they either had enlisted fraudulently or had been injured. Many of these men simply could not be Marines, but it did not mean that they were not good men.

As a Corps, it is our duty to return everyone back to society better than we receive them. What I initially saw at Casual did not please me in that regard. In too many cases, we treated these men as outcasts and dirt bags.

They were not allowed to talk, and at times, they sat straddle on a bench asshole to bellybutton at attention awaiting assignment to a working party. I told the officer in charge that I would not have it. They were young American citizens who would be returning to their homes, and it was up to us to treat them properly rather than hard-ass them out the gate. We would not coddle them but, rather, treat them properly with dignity. They would do what we said, and in return, we would treat them with respect. We would check the system so that the discharges moved as rapidly as possible.

The DIs assigned to Casual were selected for their temperament. They were not the high-stress types who constantly barked but, rather, the fatherly types who listened and talked. Duty in Casual was not considered to be choice, and yet it was critical. The recruits were considered to be trouble waiting to happen, and all sorts of stories were attributed to them. They supposedly would curse out a drill instructor in front of his platoon, make fun of the regular recruits, and all manner of things. At no time did I ever find any of these stories to be true. I believe that they were tales held over from earlier days when that perhaps was the case.

As we changed the policy, we started to receive letters from these men stating how much that they appreciated the treatment that they received. The recruiters also sent us favorable comments concerning some of these men who brought in new enlistees.

The DIs continued to press the point about not having the casuals associate with the recruits in training, so I solicited the help of the CO of

Headquarters Battalion to have the casuals eat in his mess hall. That had been in effect for several weeks when I asked one of the DIs how he felt about it.

He did not even realize that they no longer ate in the mess hall. That merely reinforced my opinion that the DIs repeated old stories about the casuals, which no longer were true.

CHAPTER 12

Why We Are Different

The recruits and DIs came into the Corps for various reasons, and yet they could not fully articulate exactly why they thought we were better that the other services. On numerous occasions, I tried to state why I thought that we were different, and to do that, I used documents to illustrate the point.

> I do solemnly swear to support and defend the constitution of the United States against all enemies foreign and domestic. That I will bear true faith and allegiance to the same. That I will obey the orders of the President of the United States and the officers appointed over me according to the rules governing the Armed Forces of the United States so help me God.

Those words are on every enlistment contract and I explained them. "Each and every one of you took that oath as he entered the Corps. That is quite different from accepting a job in any other corporation. "I do solemnly swear" and "so help me God" are very heavy words. Unlike any other profession, ours demands that we go where we are ordered, and if combat occurs, then we are expected to possibly sacrifice our lives. There are those who attempt to equate our profession to some type of civilian job. That cannot be done effectively because of all the sacrifices that are expected of us. The military is unique.

Each of you also heard the following words:

> Know ye that reposing special trust and confidence in the fidelity and abilities of ——, I do appoint him a —— in the United States Marine Corps to rank as such from the first day of March, 1984. This appointee will therefore carefully and diligently discharge the duties of the grade to which appointed by doing and performing all manner of things thereunto pertaining. And I do strictly charge

> and require all personnel of lesser grade to render obedience to appropriate orders. And this appointee is to observe and follow such orders and directions as may be given from time to time by superiors acting according to the rules and articles governing the discipline of the armed forces of the united states of america. Given under my hand at unit this first day of March, in the year of our Lord nineteen hundred and eighty-four.

Those words spell out exactly what you are expected to do concerning juniors and seniors. They give you authority for your grade and, at the same time, tell you that you must obey orders and regulations from above. Again, they are heavy words, and they are normally pronounced in front of a formation of troops so all can hear and know that you have been promoted.

In a civilian organization, one may be promoted with very little fanfare. In the Marines, we advertise promotions and ensure that all concerned realize that it is a "big deal."

At each graduation, the battalion commander speaks, and among the other things, he says, "The standards are identical, performance is what we expect, and leadership by example is practiced by every officer and drill instructor." All these words are generally the same for each of the services. The difference occurs because we not only say them but also live them. We demand that our Marines reach those standards, and if they cannot, then they cannot become or remain a Marine.

In the civilian community, there is nothing even approaching these requirements. If one does not like his job, he always has the option of leaving. You will constantly hear that Marines are different, and that is true. We start with our enlistment policy. If an individual has had difficulty with drugs, we do not want him. The same applies if he has had difficulty with the police. We send some of our very best Marines to become recruiters so that they will recruit Marines like themselves. Next comes our training in Boot Camp. We make it difficult so that we can weed out those who will not make good Marines. After you leave Boot Camp you will be constantly challenged. You will find that being a Marine is fun. It must be because we sure don't remain for the money. Don't get me wrong, the money isn't bad, but you sure won't become rich in the Corps. It will not be fun every minute of every day; you will have some bad days. That I can assure you, but overall, it will be fun.

That's why we remain. You will develop friendships, which will last for a lifetime. After a while, it will be impossible to report to a duty station without knowing someone who will go out of his way to assist you in getting settled. You will not find that as often in civilian life. Even after you depart the Corps, you remain a Marine. The country demands and expects more of its Marines. Any time that an old Marine is involved in any type of newsworthy incident, it is mentioned that he was a Marine. That does not always occur if he was a soldier, sailor, or airman. During your stay in Boot Camp, we will spend a lot of time describing the deeds of units and individuals throughout our history. What they did is one of the reasons why we remain an elite organization. "Be one of the few, one of the proudest" means a lot to all Marines and our older Marines. Americans expect nothing but the best from their Marines.

CHAPTER 13

Changes and Results

Before Major General McMonagle left as the commanding general, he asked me to make a list of the changes that we had made at the Depot during our tenure. I noted that it probably would be a long one. Later that day, I sat down and proceeded to compile such a list. It was in fact a long list, and we could be justly proud of our achievements. The following are a few of the accomplishments during more than two years.

Attitudes

There was no doubt that the attitudes of the officers and DIs did, in fact, change. One could see positive leadership being utilized on frequent occasions where, in the past, it would have been negative. The extensions of DIs requesting to remain on the field had dramatically increased, while the number having difficulties had been reduced by 67 percent.

Diary, January 25, 1984

The extensions continue to come in and they are for good DIs. We will not lose 20 DIs this year.

Continuous liaison with the operating forces showed that they were happy with the quality and discipline of the new Marines that they received. The overall non-EAS (Expiration of Active Service) attrition for the entire Corps continued to go down, as did the disciplinary rate.

The DIs seemed to be having more fun training recruits, and the number of their marital problems had ceased to rise. The DIs were more open when discussing how to make new Marines. That was a healthy sign. They actually smiled!

Stress Management

Although stress management classes had been suspended, they had been conducted, and the benefits were obvious. My new assignment would be in the training department at HQMC in the Professional Development and Education Branch where I would have staff cognizance over both depots. Perhaps there I could reinstitute it at both depots.

FTU

The field-training unit had revamped the training so that the training now flowed more logically and the recruits spent more time in the field. There was flexibility and time to recover in the event of inclement weather. Hikes had been added, and the foot problems were greatly reduced since it was developmental and progressive.

PCP

The initial strength test had been changed to give a better indication of the physical condition of the recruits when they arrived. The organization of PCP had been adjusted so that the training actually built upon success and enhanced the motivation of the recruits.

Diary, April 19, 1983

> *Visited PCP. They are really high on the new program. We sent 15 recruits back to the battalions today. The recruits also are high on the program.*

In addition to PT, the recruits learned all the Phase 1 academics and drill. Now they could be assigned to other than training day one upon return to a regular platoon. In addition to everything else, we will save money by having the PCP recruits spend less time in Boot Camp.

The failure rate at PCP went down dramatically, and many DIs no longer looked at a PCP recruit as a problem.

MRP

MRP ceased to be an additional casual platoon as we attempted to maintain motivation and teach academics along with conducting appropriate PT. Only those recruits who could return to training were allowed to remain in MRP. The others were dropped to Casual for billeting and ultimate discharge.

Casual

The recruits in Casual were treated properly and discharged more expeditiously.

Diary, July 11, 1983

The visit by the Commandant, Gen. P. X. Kelley, on 8 Jul. went well. After seeing Casual, he said that the trip would have been worth it if that were all that he saw.

Hats in Support Battalion

All DIs now wore the hats, which distinguished them as DIs, and the morale improved as a result.

Size of Platoons

The size of platoons during the summer was reduced from seventy-two to sixty, which resulted in numerous savings. It took less time to run a platoon through the mess line, academic classes, rifle range, shots, and all other evolutions. In addition, the racks could be spread apart in the squad bays, and as a result, the sickness caused by communicable diseases was greatly reduced.

It also was much easier for the DIs to train sixty recruits as compared to seventy-two, and I'm sure that this contributed to the reduced abuse.

Digging in Heels

When I initially arrived at the Regiment, the platoons were almost goose-stepping as they deliberately dug in their heels during marching. That caused an excessive number of stress fractures to the feet and did not contribute to marching properly. After it was eliminated, the doctors at the dispensary asked what had caused the dramatic reduction in stress fractures. They could see a definite change, and it pleased them since that type of fracture was difficult to treat.

Women Marines in 602

All series-size instruction was conducted in building 602 by DIs from ITU. Since a Marine would be exposed to women Marines after he left Boot Camp, it was decided that it would be a good idea if he became accustomed to seeing them during his initial training. We contacted the Women Recruit Training Command (WRTC) and asked if it could provide an instructor for such topics as first aid and other subjects not associated with combat. We screened several and selected one to be the first. It turned out quite well. Now the recruits could see that the women were, in fact, part of the team, and perhaps that would reduce difficulties later when these new Marines saw their first woman Marine.

Individual Strength Test

The initial IST required one pull-up, twenty-five sit-ups, and a mile run in ten minutes. By the time the first fitness test occurred, around training day 20, we had a sizable number who could not pass. We now had a PT problem *and* a motivation problem. The motivation problem was the bigger of the two.

We changed the IST to two pull-ups, thirty-five sit-ups, and a mile-and-a-half run. Although the initial numbers of recruits sent to PCP went up, the overall success rate for all recruits also went up since we eliminated the motivation problem.

Swimming
Diary, July 27, 1982

> *Have started several new ideas. The Operations Officer, LtCol Sortino, devised a plan to increase the number of second class swimmers and it is working.*

We initially spent a lot of time attempting to qualify everyone as a second-class swimmer. Regulations did not require this except for a few special MOSs. As a result, we did not have the time to spend with the unqualified swimmers, and many of them left as unqualified. We changed the routine so that we only tested those necessary for second class and spent the saved time teaching the unqualified swimmers how to swim. The change in statistics was dramatic.

Confidence Course

The confidence course consisted of about a dozen obstacles requiring a lot of upper-body strength. In addition, many of them were vertical obstacles, which assisted the recruits in overcoming any fear of heights that they might have.

It was not unusual for a series to be assigned to the course during its second week of training. Many were not yet strong enough to negotiate the course, and rather than it being a confidence builder, it could become a confidence buster. The schedule was changed so that a series never ran the course until at least the end of the third week and ideally not until Phase III. The number who had difficulty with the course dropped significantly, and it did become a confidence builder.

Wearing of Trousers

During prior assignments, I noticed that almost all the new Marines arriving from Boot Camp had their trousers too long. They either had them altered at government expense or their own so that they did not drag on the deck. When I went to clothing where the recruits were fitted, I discovered why. The tailors hiked the trousers up above their hips and altered them for that wear. Marines don't wear their trousers that high, and when they left Boot Camp they wore them where they normally did and they dragged on the deck. Regulations required that they be fitted at that height even though they did not wear them there. I spoke to Col. Barry Rust, the depot supply officer, and outlined the problem. It was costing the government and the Marines more money. If we changed the regulations, we would save. We contacted the supply depot at Albany and, after much bickering, received permission to change the way we fit the trousers. Chalk another one up to the good guys!

Final Drill Competition

Each battalion conducted the final drill competition within each series, and they used their own evaluators. The Regiment had no input nor did the DI school. As a result, minor variations of marching crept into the drill. In addition, it was rare for a new senior DI to be able to win the final drill. In order to ensure that we did teach the drill the same, we changed the evaluation procedure. The evaluators for the final drill consisted of the drillmaster from the battalion being evaluated, the Regimental and DI school drillmasters, and two first sergeants from the other battalions. That guaranteed that we taught the same in all the drills, and it coerced the key personnel in each battalion to see what each others did. After that was implemented, more new senior DIs starting winning the drill since favorites could not be given special consideration by the battalion evaluators. And more importantly, it assisted in improving the marching.

Professional Books

Many techniques for training or improving professionalism can be learned from books. In an effort to improve the professionalism of the officers and DIs, the Regiment had books purchased for each of the battalions. Many of the quotations that I used in the *Word* came from those books, and perhaps if they were available, they would be read and used.

Tours to Other Bases

The DIs from the two depots had been exchanging visits for years in an effort to make them duplicates of each other, taking into consideration the different climates and conditions. I attempted to expand on this by sending our DIs to such places as Recruit Training, Orlando, to see the navy training program and Basic Training, Fort Jackson, South Carolina, to see the army program so that they could compare and perhaps pick up some ideas. After seeing the other systems, they better appreciated what we had in comparison. It was amazing how many troop handlers from Fort Jackson came to Parris Island to observe our training.

Graduation Program

At each graduation, a program was issued to the families and visitors that had the names of the honor graduates and key personnel listed. However, the names of all the graduates were not listed anywhere. A friend of mine attended one of the graduations and mentioned that fact and wondered why we did not recognize each new Marine since the ceremony was in their honor. At the next graduation and every one thereafter, all the names of the graduates were listed by platoon.

The preceding examples are by no means the only changes that occurred during the twenty-six months, but they give an idea of the magnitude and results. It was a team effort in which most of the command, from recruits to DIs and officers, was involved. No area was sacrosanct, and we were not hesitant about writing to headquarters to change anything that we felt should be changed. We were supported most of the time.

When my change of command finally arrived, I could look with satisfaction at the achievements accomplished by some of the finest Marines in the Corps. Since that time, I have served with literally hundreds of former DIs and recruits and have rarely been disappointed at what I saw. Most of the changes instituted at Parris Island continued in effect years later. As was mentioned in the foreword, this is not *the* way but, rather, a way that has proven to be very effective.

One of the final actions, which I took before leaving the Regiment, was to hold one last meeting with my officers. I asked them to bring paper and pen. Among other things, I told them that I could not predict whether it would be better or worse with a new commander but that it would be different. I asked them to give him their full cooperation, loyalty, and support and to always remember that the most important thing was to train the correct way. I then asked them to write on a sheet of paper the most important things that they had learned during their tour in the Regiment and that I did not want their names. The Regiment had over one hundred officers, and it was heartwarming to read the responses. The following is an example of one of them:

> I have been fortunate to have served as the executive officer of the 1st Battalion since July 1983. Since that time I have observed numerous examples of positive leadership from you. I would say that the most important thing would be doing things right.

While this is a very broad topic, I want to provide more specific examples:

Patience. For someone who has the overwhelming responsibility of training 25,000-plus recruits each year, you have demonstrated unbelievable patience. That patience and understanding helped me to "do things right." It also builds confidence in all of us. God help us if we ever get a screamer.

Communications. I feel very comfortable in knowing that I can call on anyone in the Regiment and get assistance. Even though we are separate battalions, our communications are such that it is a "we" environment rather than the Hatfields and McCoys. This is a "doing things right" attitude.

SOP. While it is very easy to emphasize strict adherence to the SOP, you have shown us that the key is to work on attitudes of DIs as well as officers. If we can't or don't believe that the SOP is "doing things right," then we will not succeed.

Family. Recognition of the family team, particularly including the wives, has been refreshing. We seem to have lost this tradition in some organizations. It has been a tradition of "doing things right," which we have had in the Corps for some time. Thanks to you and Mrs. Myers, many of the officers have received favorable exposure to this principle or tradition, and you can feel confident that we will continue with it.

I could probably give numerous other examples of "doing things right" such as not shooting the messenger, but I believe they all fall under the general principle of "doing things right." Thank you for your support, guidance, and leadership.

Of all the responses, only one was negative, and that was from a relatively new officer who felt that as a series officer, his judgment should never be questioned if he determined that a recruit should be discharged. Since he had recent experience in the fleet, he could tell if a recruit would make a good Marine.

I felt good about turning the Regiment over and the comments merely contributed to that feeling. Approximately fifty thousand new Marines had graduated from Parris Island since I had taken command, in effect, 25 percent of the Corps! The final proof of the pudding would be when they returned as DIs. The combat aspect had already been proven since a large percentage of the Marines who served in Grenada and Lebanon had served less than one year in the Corps and had performed well.

EPILOGUE

Since leaving Parris Island, I served at Headquarters, Marine Corps, and then for over three years at Marine Barracks, Washington, DC, as the commanding officer. The Marines today are fantastic! Their only limitation is the leadership that is provided. When that leadership is present, there is nothing that they cannot do and do it to perfection.

When one praises the current Marines, some older Marines may feel that it demeans them. Nothing could be further from the truth. The deeds of our predecessors have written many heroic chapters in the history of our Corps and Nation. The present and future Marines will continue to build on those traditions.

We have learned so much in so many different areas. In sports, the training methods are much improved, and as a result, records have fallen in all areas. Technology has allowed us to do things that were unheard of in the past. The same holds true for training recruits. Discipline and pride remain, and because of that, the Corps will continue to perform to high standards.

The results of the Gulf War merely substantiate what can be done with good leadership. The military in general and the Marines in particular performed magnificently.

That did not come as a surprise to me. In fact, during Desert Shield, I briefed my employees about what they could anticipate when the fighting started.

The media spoke about the number of Iraqis who had combat experience from the war with Iran. I told my employees that that war was much like the First World War with very little innovation. I predicted that it would be a short war and that the Iraqis would be totally confused and defeated because of our ability to maneuver and innovate. Casualties on our side would not be heavy. The end result proved that what I said was the truth.

The theme in this book states that leadership is universal and a leader in one environment can lead in another if he is willing to make minor adjustments to the environment. I was the general manager of York Industries from 1989 to 1992. York Industries is an aerospace company and produces accumulators and actuators along with a few other products. It was a ten-million-dollar company that had nearly gone bankrupt. The principles used at Parris Island and all other organizations that I led with Marines were used at York. They worked equally as well.

In fact, I used the same approach with modifications when I was involved in dealing with juvenile delinquents in the Baltimore area. They work in all environments.